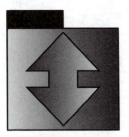

Alamance Community College
Library
P.O. Box 8000
Graham, NC 27253

Debating Points

D0145461

Alamance Community College
Library
P.O. Box 8000
Graham, NC 27253

Debating Points:
Contemporary Social Issues Series

Henry L. Tischler, Series Editor

Debating Points: Crime and Corrections
Henry L. Tischler

Debating Points: Marriage and Family Issues
Henry L. Tischler

Debating Points: Race and Ethnic Relations
Henry L. Tischler

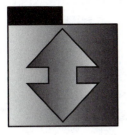

Debating Points:
Crime and Corrections

Henry L. Tischler, Editor

Framingham State College

Upper Saddle River, New Jersey 07458

Library of Congress Cataloging-in-Publication Data

Debating points: crime and corrections/Henry L. Tischler, editor.
   p. cm.—(Debating points—contemporary social issues)
   Includes bibliographical references.
   ISBN 0-13-084860-3
   1. Criminal justice, Administration of—United States.   2. Corrections—United States.
   I. Tischler, Henry L.   II. Series.
   HV9950.D43 2000
   364.973—dc21
                                   00-051650

VP, Editorial director: Laura Pearson
AVP, Publisher: Nancy Roberts
Senior acquisitions editor: Christopher DeJohn
Managing editor: Sharon Chambliss
Director of marketing: Beth Gillett Mejia
Editorial/production supervision: Kari Callaghan Mazzola
Prepress and manufacturing buyer: Mary Ann Gloriande
Electronic page makeup: Kari Callaghan Mazzola
Interior design: John P. Mazzola
Cover director: Jayne Conte

This book was set in 10/12 Meridien by Big Sky Composition
and was printed and bound by Courier Companies, Inc.
The cover was printed by Coral Graphic Services, Inc.

 © 2001 by Prentice-Hall, Inc.
A Division of Pearson Education
Upper Saddle River, New Jersey 07458

All rights reserved. No part of this book may be
reproduced, in any form or by any means,
without permission in writing from the publisher.

Printed in the United States of America
10 9 8 7 6 5 4 3 2 1

ISBN 0-13-084860-3

PRENTICE-HALL INTERNATIONAL (UK) LIMITED, *London*
PRENTICE-HALL OF AUSTRALIA PTY. LIMITED, *Sydney*
PRENTICE-HALL CANADA INC., *Toronto*
PRENTICE-HALL HISPANOAMERICANA, S.A., *Mexico*
PRENTICE-HALL OF INDIA PRIVATE LIMITED, *New Delhi*
PRENTICE-HALL OF JAPAN, INC., *Tokyo*
PEARSON EDUCATION ASIA PTE. LTD., *Singapore*
EDITORA PRENTICE-HALL DO BRASIL, LTDA., *Rio de Janeiro*

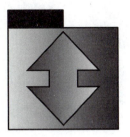

Contents

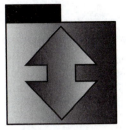

Preface

The *Debating Points: Contemporary Social Issues* series can be used to teach critical thinking, encourage student participation, and stimulate class discussion. Each book in this series is designed to provide readers with well-developed, carefully considered, and clearly written opposing viewpoints on a wide range of issues. A guiding principle in the selection of the issues for all *Debating Points* books is that they be easily understood and relevant to the backgrounds and interests of the students. Each issue within each book is self-contained and may be assigned according to the individual instructor's preferences or the dictates of classroom time.

The debate format used in each book in the *Debating Points* series helps students to understand the significance of the principles, concepts, and theories they are learning in class. It encourages students to apply critical thinking techniques to the opinions and statements they see and hear around them. Students will see that some issues do not have "right" or "wrong" answers, and that it is important to grasp the different points of view in order to gain a fuller understanding of the issue. The purpose of the debate format is to stimulate interest in the subject matter and to encourage the application of concepts and ideas. The "yes" and "no" essays have been selected to reflect a variety of ideological viewpoints and have been edited to present the views in a concise and interesting manner. The authors of the essay selections have been chosen because they are creditable scholars or commentators who are respected in their fields.

In this third volume in the *Debating Points* series—*Debating Points: Crime and Corrections*—each issue begins with an introduction that sets the stage for the debate by putting the issue into the context of a larger social science discussion and provides a brief description of the articles. Each debate concludes with a list of websites that students can research for further information on the issue. The websites have been chosen to reflect the diversity of views presented in the readings. With the advent of new communication technologies and the growing awareness of the World Wide Web, students are being exposed more frequently to differing viewpoints and sometimes questionable information. In order to process this information effectively, students are going to have to rely on their critical thinking skills. Combining the issue articles with corresponding websites allows students to continue to explore the issues for a fuller understanding.

Many instructors have recognized the importance of applying the material that has been discussed in the classroom. The *Debating Points* series is an excellent tool for encouraging students to critically evaluate the utility of various theoretical perspectives. The push is on for educators to help students strengthen their critical thinking skills. The books in the *Debating Points* series are excellent tools for teaching critical thinking in that they expose students to a variety of viewpoints and strongly argued positions related to their field of study.

Henry L. Tischler, Series Editor
txtbks@aol.com

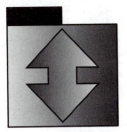

About the Contributors

HUGO ADAM BEDAU is Fletcher Professor of Philosophy at Tufts University. He has written and edited a number of books on political philosophy and on capital punishment, including *Death Is Different* (1987) and *The Death Penalty in America: Current Controversies* (1997).

DAVID GELERNTER, a professor of computer science at Yale, was letter-bombed in June 1993 and nearly lost his life. He is the author, most recently, of *Drawing Life: Surviving the Unabomber* (1997) and *Machine Beauty: Elegance and the Heart of Technology* (1998). He is currently at work on a novel.

JOSHUA WOLF SHENK is a former staff writer at *U.S. News and World Report*. He lives in Washington, D.C.

JAMES INCIARDI is a professor at the University of Delaware. He is the director of the Center for Drug and Alcohol Studies. Among his books are *Historical Approaches to Crime: Research Strategies and Issues* (1997); *The Drug Legalization Debate* (1991); *Drug Treatment and Criminal Justice* (1993); *Street Kids, Street Drugs, Street Crime: An Examination of Drug Use and Serious Delinquency in Miami* (1993); *Women and Crack Cocaine* (1993); *Drug Abuse Treatment: The Implementation of Innovative Approaches* (1994); *Sex, Drugs, and the Continuing Spread of Aids* (1995).

CHRISTINE SAUM is affiliated with the Center for Drug and Alcohol Studies at the University of Delaware.

STEVE H. HANKE is professor of applied economics at Johns Hopkins University.

HOWARD BAETJER JR. is adjunct professor of economics at the Program on Social and Organizational Learning at George Mason University and also at Loyola College in Maryland. His main research interest is the role of capital structure evolution in economic growth.

CRAIG HANEY is a professor at the University of California at Santa Cruz. His research has involved the individual and psychological adjustment to incarceration, as well as the study of the social histories of persons convicted of violent crimes.

PHIL ZIMBARDO is a psychology professor at Stanford University. His most notable study was the 1971 Stanford Prison Experiment, which was a classic demonstration of the power of social situations to distort student identities and long-cherished values when they were assigned roles as prisoners and guards. His books include *Psychology and Life* (15th ed.) with R. Gerrig (1999); *The Psychology of Attitude Change and Social Influence* with M. Leippe (1991); *The Shy Child* with S. L. Radl (1981); and *Psychology* (2nd ed.) with A. L. Weber (1997).

BYRON M. ROTH is a professor of psychology at Dowling College in Oakdale, New York. He is coauthor (with John D. Mullen) of *Decision Making: Its Logic and Practice* (1990) and *Prescription for Failure: Race Relations in the Age of Social Science* (1994).

HERBERT WRAY writes for *U.S. News and World Report*.

DOUGLAS WEIL is director of research at the Center to Prevent Handgun Violence in Washington, D.C.

GARY KLECK is a professor at Florida State University. He is the author of *Point Blank: Guns and Violence in America* (1991), winner of the Michael Hindelang Award.

JAMES WOOTTON is founder and president of the Safe Streets Coalition, created to reduce violent crime. He helped draft the Truth in Sentencing Amendment passed by the House of Representatives in 1995. He served as deputy administrator of the Office of Juvenile Justice and Delinquency Prevention at the U.S. Department of Justice during the Reagan administration.

ROBERT O. HECK is a partner in the law firm Moore, Bieck, Heck & Associates. He was SHOCAP Project Manager from 1982 to 1994.

DAVID C. ANDERSON is author of *Sensible Justice: Alternatives to Prison* (1997) and *Crime and the Politics of Hysteria: How the Willie Horton Story Changed American Justice* (1995).

JOSEPH BESSETTE is a professor at Claremont McKenna College. He is the author of *American Government and Politics*, with John Pitney (1998).

DAVID B. KOPEL is research director of the Independence Institute in Golden, Colorado. He is the former assistant attorney general of Colorado.

ARCH PUDDINGTON is vice president for research at Freedom House. His history of Radio Free Europe–Radio Liberty is forthcoming from the University of Kentucky Press.

RANDALL KENNEDY is a professor at Harvard Law School. He was a law clerk for Justice Thurgood Marshall of the Supreme Court of the United States. He is the editor of *Reconstruction* and writes frequently on racial matters in law journals and general publications. He is the author of *Race, Crime, and the Law* (1997).

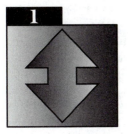

Should the Death Penalty Be Abolished?

Capital punishment has been opposed for many years and for many reasons. In the United States, the Quakers were the first to oppose the death penalty and to support providing prison sentences instead. Amnesty International, U.S.A., calls capital punishment a "horrifying lottery" in which the penalty is death and the odds of escaping are determined more by politics, money, race, and geography than by the crime committed. The group bases its impression on the fact that black men are more likely to be executed than white men, and that southern states including Texas, Virginia, Missouri, Louisiana, and Florida account for the vast majority of executions that have taken place since 1977.

It is also no fluke that nearly all death-row inmates are poor. They often had a public defender who might not have been qualified for the task. Even if the inmate's attorney made errors during the defense, the defendant's appellate attorney must demonstrate that the defense counsel's blunders directly affected the jury's verdict and that without those mistakes the jury would have returned a different verdict. One study (Radelet, Bedau, and Putnam, 1992), for instance, found that between 1900 and 1991, 416 innocent people were convicted of capital crimes and 23 actually were executed. The two most frequent causes of errors that produced wrongful convictions were perjury by prosecution witnesses and mistaken eyewitness testimony.

People also argue that the death penalty is applied in a racially discriminatory fashion. One extensive study (Baldus, Woodworth, and Pulaski Jr., 1990) concluded that the odds of being condemned to death were 4.3 times greater for defendants who killed whites than for defendants who killed blacks. Opponents of the death penalty have used this information to make the case that it should be abolished entirely on the grounds that racial bias is

1

an inevitable part of the administration of capital punishment in the United States and that it would be better to have no death penalty than one influenced by prejudice. Others argue that the remedy to the problem is to do what is known as leveling up by increasing the number of people executed for murdering blacks. They argue that if we sentence more murderers of black people to death then we are eliminating the bias. Another solution would be to impose mandatory death sentences for certain types of crimes. In this way we would eliminate discretionary judgments and the potential for bias (Kennedy, 1997).

Hugo Adam Bedau, in "The Case against the Death Penalty," notes that capital punishment does not deter crime, and the death penalty is uncivilized in theory and unfair and inequitable in practice. He points out that 28 European countries have abolished the death penalty either in law or in practice. Canada abolished it in 1976. The unmistakable worldwide trend is toward the complete abolition of capital punishment. Countries that make use of capital punishment are known for their disregard for the human rights of their citizens: China, Iraq, Iran, South Africa, and the former Soviet Union. He feels that Americans should be embarrassed to find themselves linked with the governments of such nations in retaining execution as a method of crime control.

David Gelernter, in "What Do Murderers Deserve?," believes that in executing murderers we declare that deliberate murder is absolutely evil and absolutely intolerable. When a murder takes place the community is obliged, whether it feels like it or not, to clear its throat and step up to the microphone. Every murder demands a communal response. Among possible responses, the death penalty is uniquely powerful because it is permanent and can never be retracted or overturned. An execution forces the community to assume forever the burden of moral certainty; it is a form of absolute speech that allows no waffling or equivocation. Deliberate murder, the community announces, is absolutely evil and absolutely intolerable, period. Gelernter notes that communities may exist in which capital punishment is no longer the necessary response to deliberate murder, but, he feels, America today is not one of them.

The Case against the Death Penalty

Hugo Adam Bedau

Introduction

In 1972, the Supreme Court declared that under then existing laws "the imposition and carrying out of the death penalty ... constitutes cruel and unusual punishment in violation of the Eighth and Fourteenth Amendments." (*Furman v. Georgia*, 408 U.S. 238) The majority of the Court concentrated its objections on the way death penalty laws had been applied, finding the result so "harsh, freakish, and arbitrary" as to be constitutionally unacceptable. Making the nationwide impact of its decision unmistakable, the Court summarily reversed death sentences in the many cases then before it, which involved a wide range of state statutes, crimes, and factual situations.

But within four years after the *Furman* decision, more than 600 persons had been sentenced to death under new capital punishment statutes that provided guidance for the jury's sentencing discretion. These statutes typically require a bifurcated (two-stage) trial procedure, in which the jury first determines guilt or innocence and then chooses imprisonment or death in the light of aggravating or mitigating circumstances.

In July 1976, the Supreme Court moved in the opposite direction, holding that "the punishment of death does not invariably violate the Constitution." The Court ruled that these new statutes contained "objective standards to guide, regularize, and make rationally reviewable the process for imposing the sentence of death." (*Gregg v. Georgia*, 428 U.S. 153) Thus

Copyright © 1992 by Hugo Adam Bedau. Reprinted with the permission of the author and the American Civil Liberties Union.

the states as well as Congress have had for some years constitutionally valid statutory models for death penalty laws, and more than three dozen state legislatures have enacted death penalty statutes patterned after those the Court upheld in *Gregg*. In recent years, Congress has enacted death penalty statutes for peacetime espionage by military personnel and for drug-related murders.

Executions resumed in 1977, and by the early 1990s nearly three thousand persons were under sentence of death and more than 180 had been executed.

Despite the Supreme Court's 1976 ruling in *Gregg v. Georgia*, the American Civil Liberties Union (ACLU) continues to oppose capital punishment on moral and practical, as well as on constitutional, grounds:

- Capital punishment is cruel and unusual. It is a relic of the earliest days of penology, when slavery, branding, and other corporal punishments were commonplace. Like those other barbaric practices, executions have no place in a civilized society.

- Opposition to the death penalty does not arise from misplaced sympathy for convicted murderers. On the contrary, murder demonstrates a lack of respect for human life. For this very reason, murder is abhorrent, and any policy of state-authorized killings is immoral.

- Capital punishment denies due process of law. Its imposition is arbitrary and irrevocable. It forever deprives an individual of benefits of new evidence or new law that might warrant the reversal of a conviction or the setting aside of a death sentence.

- The death penalty violates the constitutional guarantee of the equal protection of the laws. It is applied randomly at best and discriminatorily at worst. It is imposed disproportionately upon those whose victims are white, on offenders who are people of color, and on those who are themselves poor and uneducated.

- The defects in death penalty laws, conceded by the Supreme Court in the early 1970s, have not been appreciably altered by the shift from unfettered discretion to "guided discretion." These changes in death sentencing have proved to be largely cosmetic. They merely mask the impermissible arbitrariness of a process that results in an execution.

- Executions give society the unmistakable message that human life no longer deserves respect when it is useful to take it and that homicide is legitimate when deemed justified by pragmatic concerns.

- Reliance on the death penalty obscures the true causes of crime and distracts attention from the social measures that effectively contribute to its control. Politicians who preach the desirability of executions as a weapon of crime control deceive the public and mask their own failure to support anti-crime measures that will really work.

- Capital punishment wastes resources. It squanders the time and energy of courts, prosecuting attorneys, defense counsel, juries, and courtroom and correctional personnel. It unduly burdens the system of criminal justice, and it is therefore counterproductive as an instrument for society's control of violent crime. It epitomizes the tragic inefficacy and brutality of the resort to violence rather than reason for the solution of difficult social problems.

- A decent and humane society does not deliberately kill human beings. An execution is a dramatic, public spectacle of official, violent homicide that teaches the permissibility of killing people to solve social problems—the worst possible example to set for society. In this century, governments have too often attempted to justify their lethal fury by the benefits such killing would bring to the rest of society. The bloodshed is real and deeply destructive of the common decency of the community; the benefits are illusory.

Two conclusions buttress our entire case: Capital punishment does not deter crime, and the death penalty is uncivilized in theory and unfair and inequitable in practice.

Deterrence

The argument most often cited in support of capital punishment is that the threat of executions deters capital crimes more effectively than imprisonment. This claim is plausible, but the facts do not support it. The death penalty fails as a deterrent for several reasons:

1. Any punishment can be an effective deterrent only if it is consistently and promptly employed. Capital punishment cannot be administered to meet these conditions.

   Only a small proportion of first-degree murderers is sentenced to death, and even fewer are executed. Although death sentences since 1980 have increased in number to about 250 per year, this is still only 1 percent of all homicides known to the police. Of all those convicted on a charge of criminal homicide, only 2 percent—about 1 in 50—are eventually sentenced to death.

   ...

2. Persons who commit murder and other crimes of personal violence either premeditate them or they do not. If the crime is premeditated, the criminal ordinarily concentrates on escaping detection, arrest, and conviction. The threat of even the severest punishment will not deter those who expect to escape detection and arrest. If the crime is not premeditated, then it is impossible to imagine how the threat

of any punishment could deter it. Most capital crimes are committed during moments of great emotional stress or under the influence of drugs or alcohol, when logical thinking has been suspended. Impulsive or expressive violence is inflicted by persons heedless of the consequences to themselves as well as to others.

Gangland killings, air piracy, drive-by shootings, and kidnapping for ransom are among the graver felonies that continue to be committed because some individuals think they are too clever to get caught. Political terrorism is usually committed in the name of an ideology that honors its martyrs; trying to cope with it by threatening death for terrorists is futile.... Anyone trafficking in illegal drugs is already betting his life in violent competition with other dealers. It is irrational to think that the death penalty—a remote threat at best—will deter murders committed in drug turf wars or by street-level dealers.

3. If, however, severe punishment can deter crime, then long-term imprisonment is severe enough to cause any rational person not to commit violent crimes. The vast preponderance of the evidence shows that the death penalty is no more effective than imprisonment in deterring murder and that it may even be an incitement to criminal violence in certain cases.

- Death penalty states as a group do not have lower rates of criminal homicide than non-death penalty states.
- Use of the death penalty in a given state may increase the subsequent rate of criminal homicide in that state.
- In neighboring states—one with the death penalty and the others without it—the one with the death penalty does not show a consistently lower rate of criminal homicide.
- Police officers on duty do not suffer a higher rate of criminal assault and homicide in states that have abolished the death penalty than they do in death penalty states.
- Prisoners and prison personnel do not suffer a higher rate of criminal assault and homicide from life-term prisoners in abolition states than they do in death penalty states.

...

Furthermore, cases have been clinically documented where the death penalty actually incited the capital crimes it was supposed to deter. These include instances of the so-called suicide-by-execution syndrome—persons who wanted but feared to take their own life and committed murder so that society would kill them.

It must, of course, be conceded that inflicting the death penalty guarantees that the condemned person will commit no further crimes. This is an incapacitative, not a deterrent, effect of executions. Furthermore, it is too high a price to pay when studies show that very few convicted murderers ever commit another crime of violence.

...

Recidivism among murderers does occasionally happen. But it happens less frequently than most people believe; the media rarely distinguish between a paroled murderer who murders again and other murderers who have a previous criminal record but not for homicide.

There is no way to predict which convicted murderers will kill again. Repeat murders could be prevented only by executing all those convicted of criminal homicide. Such a policy is too inhumane and brutal to be taken seriously. Society would never tolerate dozens of executions daily, yet nothing less would suffice. Equally effective but far less inhumane is a policy of life imprisonment without the possibility of parole.

Unfairness

Constitutional due process as well as elementary justice require that the judicial functions of trial and sentencing be conducted with fundamental fairness, especially where the irreversible sanction of the death penalty is involved. In murder cases (since 1930, 99 percent of all executions have been for this crime), there has been substantial evidence to show that courts have been arbitrary, racially biased, and unfair in the way in which they have sentenced some persons to prison but others to death.

Racial discrimination was one of the grounds on which the Supreme Court relied in *Furman* in ruling the death penalty unconstitutional.

...

The nation's death rows have always had a disproportionately large population of African Americans, relative to their fraction of the total population.

...

Since the revival of the death penalty in the mid-1970s, about half of those on death row at any given time have been black—a disproportionately large fraction given the black/white ratio of the total population, but not so obviously unfair if judged by the fact that roughly 50 percent of all those arrested for murder were also black. Nevertheless, when those under death sentence are examined more closely, it turns out that race is a decisive factor after all.

An exhaustive statistical study of racial discrimination in capital cases in Georgia, for example, showed that "the average odds of receiving a death sentence among all indicted cases were 4.3 times higher in cases with white victims." In 1987 these data were placed before the Supreme Court in *McCleskey v. Kemp* and the Court did not dispute the statistical evidence. The

Court did hold, however, that the evidence failed to show that there was "a constitutionally significant risk of racial bias...." (481 U.S. 279)

In 1990, the U.S. General Accounting Office reported to the Congress the results of its review of empirical studies on racism and the death penalty. The GAO concluded: "Our synthesis of the 28 studies shows a pattern of evidence indicating racial disparities in the charging, sentencing, and imposition of the death penalty after the *Furman* decision" and that "race of victim influence was found at all stages of the criminal justice system process...."

These results cannot be explained away by relevant nonracial factors (such as prior criminal record or type of crime), and they lead to a very unsavory conclusion: In the trial courts of this nation, even at the present time, the killing of a white is treated much more severely than the killing of a black.

...

Discrimination against the poor (and in our society racial minorities are disproportionately poor) is also well established. "Approximately 90 percent of those on death row could not afford to hire a lawyer when they were tried." A defendant's poverty, lack of firm social roots in the community, inadequate legal representation at trial or on appeal—all these have been common factors among death-row populations. As Justice William O. Douglas noted in *Furman*, "One searches our chronicles in vain for the execution of any member of the affluent strata in this society." (408 U.S. 238)

The demonstrated inequities in the actual administration of capital punishment should tip the balance against it in the judgment of fair-minded and impartial observers. "Whatever else might be said for the use of death as a punishment, one lesson is clear from experience: This is a power that we cannot exercise fairly and without discrimination."

...

Inevitability of Error

Unlike all other criminal punishments, the death penalty is uniquely irrevocable. Speaking to the French Chamber of Deputies in 1830, years after the excesses of the French Revolution, which he had witnessed, the Marquis de Lafayette said, "I shall ask for the abolition of the punishment of death until I have the infallibility of human judgment demonstrated to me." Although some proponents of capital punishment would argue that its merits are worth the occasional execution of innocent people, most would also insist that there is little likelihood of the innocent being executed. Yet a large body of evidence shows that innocent people are often convicted of crimes, including capital crimes, and that some of them have been executed.

Since 1900, in this country, there have been on the average more than four cases per year in which an entirely innocent person was convicted of murder. Scores of these persons were sentenced to death. In many cases, a reprieve or commutation arrived just hours, or even minutes, before the scheduled execution. These erroneous convictions have occurred in virtually every jurisdiction from one end of the nation to the other. Nor have they declined in recent years, despite the new death penalty statutes approved by the Supreme Court.

...

Barbarity

The traditional mode of execution, still available in a few states, is hanging. Death on the gallows is easily bungled: If the drop is too short, there will be a slow and agonizing death by strangulation. If the drop is too long, the head will be torn off.

Two states, Idaho and Utah, still authorize the firing squad. The prisoner is strapped into a chair, and hooded. A target is pinned to the chest. Five marksmen, one with blanks, take aim and fire.

Electrocution has been the most widely used form of execution in this country in this century. The condemned prisoner is led—or dragged—into the death chamber, strapped into the chair, and electrodes are fastened to the head and legs. When the switch is thrown the body strains, jolting as the voltage is raised and lowered. Often smoke rises from the head. There is the awful odor of burning flesh. No one knows how long electrocuted individuals retain consciousness.

...

An attempt to improve on electrocution was the gas chamber. The prisoner is strapped into a chair, a container of sulfuric acid underneath. The chamber is sealed, and cyanide is dropped into the acid to form lethal gas.

...

The latest mode of inflicting the death penalty, enacted into law by nearly two dozen states, is lethal injection, first used in Texas in 1982. It is easy to overstate the humaneness and efficacy of this method. There is no way of knowing that it is really painless. As the U.S. Court of Appeals observed, there is "substantial and uncontroverted evidence ... that execution by lethal injection poses a serious risk of cruel, protracted death.... Even a slight error in dosage or administration can leave a prisoner conscious but paralyzed while dying, a sentient witness of his or her own asphyxiation." (*Chaney v. Heckler*, 718 F.2d 1174 [1983])

...

Indeed, by its veneer of decency and by subtle analogy with life-saving medical practice, death by lethal injection makes killing as punishment more acceptable to the public. Even when it prevents the struggles of the condemned person and avoids maiming the body, it is no different from hanging or shooting as an expression of the absolute power of the state over the helpless individual.

...

Retribution

Justice, it is often insisted, requires the death penalty as the only suitable retribution for heinous crimes. This claim will not bear scrutiny. All punishment by its nature is retributive, not only the death penalty. Whatever legitimacy, therefore, is to be found in punishment as just retribution can in principle be satisfied without recourse to executions.

It is also obvious that the death penalty could be defended on narrowly retributive grounds only for the crime of murder, and not for any of the many other crimes that have frequently been made subject to this mode of punishment (rape, kidnapping, espionage, treason, drug kingpins). Few defenders of the death penalty are willing to confine themselves consistently to the narrow scope afforded by retribution.

...

It is also often argued that death is what murderers deserve, and that those who oppose the death penalty violate the fundamental principle that criminals should be punished according to their deserts—"making the punishment fit the crime."

If this principle is understood to require that punishments are unjust unless they are like the crime itself, then the principle is unacceptable. It would require us to rape rapists, torture torturers, and inflict other horrible and degrading punishments on offenders. It would require us to betray traitors and kill multiple murderers again and again, punishments impossible to inflict. Since we cannot reasonably aim to punish all crimes according to this principle, it is arbitrary to invoke it as a requirement of justice in the punishment of murderers.

If, however, the principle of just deserts is understood to require that the severity of punishments must be proportional to the gravity of the crime, and that murder being the gravest crime deserves the severest punishment, then the principle is no doubt sound. But it does not compel support for the death penalty. What it does require is that crimes other than murder be punished with terms of imprisonment or other deprivations less severe than those used in the punishment of murder.

Criminals no doubt deserve to be punished, and punished with severity appropriate to their culpability and the harm they have caused to the innocent. But severity of punishment has its limits—imposed both by justice and our common human dignity. Governments that respect these limits do not use premeditated, violent homicide as an instrument of social policy.

...

Financial Costs

It is sometimes suggested that abolishing capital punishment is unfair to the taxpayer, as though life imprisonment were obviously more expensive than executions. If one takes into account all the relevant costs, the reverse is true. "The death penalty is not now, nor has it ever been, a more economical alternative to life imprisonment."

A murder trial normally takes much longer when the death penalty is at issue than when it is not. Litigation costs—including the time of judges, prosecutors, public defenders, and court reporters, and the high costs of briefs—are all borne by the taxpayer.

A 1982 study showed that, were the death penalty to be reintroduced in New York, the cost of the capital trial alone would be more than double the cost of a life term in prison.

...

Florida, with one of the nation's largest death rows, has estimated that the true cost of each execution is approximately $3.2 million, or approximately six times the cost of a life-imprisonment sentence.

...

Public Opinion

The media commonly report that the American public overwhelmingly supports the death penalty. More careful analysis of public attitudes, however, reveals that most Americans would oppose the death penalty if convicted murderers were sentenced to life without parole and were required to make some form of financial restitution.

...

Abolition Trends

The death penalty in the United States needs to be put into international perspective. In 1962, it was reported to the Council of Europe that "the facts clearly show that the death penalty is regarded in Europe as something of an anachronism...."

Today, 28 European countries have abolished the death penalty either in law or in practice. In Great Britain, it was abolished (except for treason) in 1971; France abolished it in 1981. Canada abolished it in 1976. The United Nations General Assembly affirmed in a formal resolution that, throughout the world, it is desirable to "progressively restrict the number of offenses for which the death penalty might be imposed, with a view to the desirability of abolishing this punishment."

Conspicuous by their indifference to these recommendations are nations generally known for their disregard for the human rights of their citizens: China, Iraq, Iran, South Africa, and the former Soviet Union. Americans ought to be embarrassed to find themselves linked with the governments of such nations in retaining execution as a method of crime control.

...

The unmistakable worldwide trend is toward the complete abolition of capital punishment.

No

David
Gelernter

What Do Murderers Deserve?

No civilized nation ever takes the death penalty for granted; two recent cases force us to consider it yet again. A Texas woman, Karla Faye Tucker, murdered two people with a pickaxe, was said to have repented in prison, and was put to death. A Montana man, Theodore Kaczynski, murdered three people with mail bombs, did not repent, and struck a bargain with the Justice Department; he pleaded guilty and will not be executed. (He also attempted to murder others and succeeded in wounding some, myself included.) Why did we execute the penitent and spare the impenitent? However we answer this question, we surely have a duty to ask it.

...

Why execute murderers? To deter? To avenge? Supporters of the death penalty often give the first answer, opponents the second. But neither can be the whole truth. If our main goal were deterring crime, we would insist on public executions—which are not on the political agenda, and not an item that many Americans are interested in promoting. If our main goal were vengeance, we would allow the grieving parties to decide the murderer's fate; if the victim had no family or friends to feel vengeful on his behalf, we would call the whole thing off.

In fact, we execute murderers in order to make a communal proclamation: that murder is intolerable. A deliberate murderer embodies evil so terrible that it defiles the community. Thus the late social philosopher Robert Nisbet: "Until a catharsis has been effected through trial, through the finding of guilt and then punishment, the community is anxious, fearful, apprehensive, and above all, contaminated."

From *Commentary* (April 1998). Copyright © 1999. Reprinted with the permission of the author and *Commentary*. All rights reserved.

Individual citizens have a right and sometimes a duty to speak. A community has the right, too, and sometimes the duty. The community certifies births and deaths, creates marriages, educates children, fights invaders. In laws, deeds, and ceremonies it lays down the boundary lines of civilized life, lines that are constantly getting scuffed and needing renewal.

When a murder takes place, the community is obliged, whether it feels like it or not, to clear its throat and step up to the microphone. Every murder demands a communal response. Among possible responses, the death penalty is uniquely powerful because it is permanent and can never be retracted or overturned. An execution forces the community to assume forever the burden of moral certainty; it is a form of absolute speech that allows no waffling or equivocation. Deliberate murder, the community announces, is absolutely evil and absolutely intolerable, period.

Of course, we could make the same point less emphatically if we wanted to—for example, by locking up murderers for life (as we sometimes do). The question then becomes: Is the death penalty overdoing it? Should we make a less forceful proclamation instead?

The answer might be yes if we were a community in which murder was a shocking anomaly and thus in effect a solved problem. But we are not. Our big cities are full of murderers at large. "One can guesstimate," writes the criminologist and political scientist John J. DiIulio Jr., "that we are nearing or may already have passed the day when 500,000 murderers, convicted and undetected, are living in American society."

DiIulio's statistics show an approach to murder so casual as to be depraved. We are reverting to a pre-civilized state of nature. Our natural bent in the face of murder is not to avenge the crime but to shrug it off, except in those rare cases when our own near and dear are involved. (And even then, it depends.)

This is an old story. Cain murders Abel and is brought in for questioning: Where is Abel, your brother? The suspect's response: How should I know? "What *am* I, my brother's keeper?" It is one of the very first statements attributed to mankind in the Bible; voiced here by an interested party, it nonetheless expresses a powerful and universal inclination. Why mess in other people's problems? And murder is always, in the most immediate sense, someone else's problem, because the injured party is dead.

Murder in primitive societies called for a private settling of scores. The community as a whole stayed out of it. For murder to count, as it does in the Bible, as a crime not merely against one man but against the whole community and against God—that was a moral triumph that is still basic to our integrity, and that is never to be taken for granted. By executing murderers, the community reaffirms this moral understanding by restating the truth that absolute evil exists and must be punished.

Granted (some people say), the death penalty is a communal proclamation; it is nevertheless an incoherent one. If our goal is to affirm that human life is more precious than anything else, how can we make such a declaration by destroying life?

But declaring that human life is more precious than anything else is not our goal in imposing the death penalty. Nor is the proposition true. The founding fathers pledged their lives (and fortunes and sacred honor) to the cause of freedom; Americans have traditionally believed that some things are more precious than life.... The point of capital punishment is not to pronounce on life in general but on the crime of murder.

Which is not to say that the sanctity of human life does not enter the picture. Taking a life, says the Talmud (in the course of discussing Cain and Abel), is equivalent to destroying a whole world. The rabbis used this statement to make a double point: to tell us why murder is the gravest of crimes, and to warn against false testimony in a murder trial. But to believe in the sanctity of human life does not mean, and the Talmud does not say it means, that capital punishment is ruled out.

A newer objection grows out of the seemingly random way in which we apply capital punishment. The death penalty might be a reasonable communal proclamation in principle, some critics say, but it has become so garbled in practice that it has lost all significance and ought to be dropped. DiIulio writes that "the ratio of persons murdered to persons executed for murder from 1977 to 1996 was in the ballpark of 1,000 to 1"; the death penalty has become in his view "arbitrary and capricious," a "state lottery" that is "unjust both as a matter of Judeo-Christian ethics and as a matter of American citizenship."

We can grant that, on the whole, we are doing a disgracefully bad job of administering the death penalty. After all, we are divided and confused on the issue. The community at large is strongly in favor of capital punishment; the cultural elite is strongly against it. Our attempts to speak with assurance as a community come out sounding in consequence like a man who is fighting off a chokehold as he talks. But a community as cavalier about murder as we are has no right to back down. That we are botching things does not entitle us to give up.

Opponents of capital punishment tend to describe it as a surrender to our emotions—to grief, rage, fear, blood lust. For most supporters of the death penalty, this is exactly false. Even when we resolve in principle to go ahead, we have to steel ourselves. Many of us would find it hard to kill a dog, much less a man. Endorsing capital punishment means not that we yield to our emotions but that we overcome them.... If we favor executing murderers it is not because we want to but because, however much we do *not* want to, we consider ourselves obliged to.

Many Americans, of course, no longer feel that obligation. The death penalty is hard for us as a community above all because of our moral evasiveness. For at least a generation, we have urged one another to switch off our moral faculties. "Don't be judgmental!" We have said it so many times, we are starting to believe it.

...

Our refusal to look evil in the face is no casual notion; it is a powerful drive. Thus we have (for example) the terrorist Theodore Kaczynski, who planned and carried out a hugely complex campaign of violence with a clear goal in mind. It was the goal most terrorists have: to get famous and not die. He wanted public attention for his ideas about technology; he figured he could get it by attacking people with bombs.

He was right. His plan succeeded. It is hard to imagine a more compelling proof of mental competence than this planning and carrying out over decades of a complex, rational strategy. (Evil, yes; irrational, no; they are different things.) The man himself has said repeatedly that he is perfectly sane, knew what he was doing, and is proud of it.

To call such a man insane seems to me like deliberate perversity. But many people do. Some of them insist that his thoughts about technology constitute "delusions," though every terrorist holds strong beliefs that are wrong, and many nonterrorists do, too. Some insist that sending bombs through the mail is *ipso facto* proof of insanity—as if the twentieth century had not taught us that there is no limit to the bestiality of which sane men are capable.

Where does this perversity come from? I said earlier that the community at large favors the death penalty, but intellectuals and the cultural elite tend to oppose it. This is not (I think) because they abhor killing more than other people do, but because the death penalty represents absolute speech from a position of moral certainty, and doubt is the black-lung disease of the intelligentsia—an occupational hazard now inflicted on the culture as a whole.

American intellectuals have long differed from the broader community—particularly on religion, crime and punishment, education, family, the sexes, race relations, American history, taxes and public spending, the size and scope of government, art, the environment, and the military. (Otherwise, I suppose, they and the public have been in perfect accord.) But not until the late '60s and '70s were intellectuals finally in a position to act on their convictions. Whereupon they attacked the community's moral certainties with the enthusiasm of guard dogs leaping at throats. The result is an American community smitten with the disease of intellectual doubt—or, in this case, self-doubt.

...

Returning then to the penitent woman and the impenitent man: The Karla Faye Tucker case is the harder of the two. We are told that she repented of the vicious murders she committed. If that is true, we would still have had no business forgiving her, or forgiving any murderer. As Dennis Prager has written apropos this case, only the victim is entitled to forgive, and the victim is silent. But showing mercy to penitents is part of our religious tradition, and I cannot imagine renouncing it categorically.

Why was Cain not put to death, but condemned instead to wander the earth forever? Among the answers given by the rabbis in the Midrash is that he repented. The moral category of repentance is so important, they said, that it was created before the world itself. I would therefore consider myself morally obligated to think long and hard before executing a penitent. But a true penitent would have to have renounced (as Karla Faye Tucker did) all legal attempts to overturn the original conviction. If every legal avenue has been tried and has failed, the penitence window is closed. Of course, this still leaves the difficult problem of telling counterfeit penitence from the real thing, but everything associated with capital punishment is difficult.

As for Kaczynski, the prosecutors who accepted the murderer's plea-bargain say they got the best outcome they could, under the circumstances, and I believe them. But I also regard this failure to execute a cold-blooded impenitent terrorist murderer as a tragic abdication of moral responsibility. The tragedy lies in what, under our confused system, the prosecutors felt compelled to do. The community was called on to speak unambiguously. It flubbed its lines, shrugged its shoulders, and walked away.

Which brings me back to our moral condition as a community. I can describe our plight better in artistic than in philosophical terms. The most vivid illustrations I know of self-doubt and its consequences are the paintings and sculptures of Alberto Giacometti (who died in 1966). Giacometti was an artist of great integrity; he was consumed by intellectual and moral self-doubt, which he set down faithfully. His sculpted figures show elongated, shriveled human beings who seem corroded by acid, eaten-up to the bone, hurt and weakened past fragility nearly to death. They are painful to look at. And they are natural emblems of modern America. We ought to stick one on top of the Capitol and think it over.

In executing murderers, we declare that deliberate murder is absolutely evil and absolutely intolerable. This is a painfully difficult proclamation for a self-doubting community to make. But we dare not stop trying. Communities may exist in which capital punishment is no longer the necessary response to deliberate murder. America today is not one of them.

KEY WEBSITES

COURTTV LIBRARY: THE DEATH PENALTY

This very useful site contains a history of the death penalty and general statistics. It also includes information on executions since 1976 by method, and a state-by-state legal look at capital punishment, with a handy map for information on how individual jurisdictions handle the issue. There are links to articles and analysis of the topic.
http://www.courttv.com/map/library/capital

ETHICS UPDATE—PUNISHMENT AND THE DEATH PENALTY

This site examines punishment in general and capital punishment in particular. Included are links to court decisions, legislation, statistical information, and information about other death penalty sites. The site also contains PowerPoint presentations.
http://ethics.acusd.edu/death_penalty.html

THE DEATH PENALTY—AN ONLINE SEMINAR

This extensive site created by Professor David J. W. Vanderhoof of the University of North Carolina at Pembroke has dozens of links, as well as audio versions of the professor's lectures on the topic. The site also includes tables, charts, figures, and essays about the death penalty.
http://www.uncp.edu/home/vanderhoof/death.html

ANATOMY OF A MURDER: A TRIP THROUGH OUR NATION'S LEGAL JUSTICE SYSTEM

This is a website that puts you right in the middle of the action in a criminal murder trial. You will be able to follow the story of a defendant as he faces one of the most serious charges that the legal justice system of the United States of America can levy against an individual. Absolutely every aspect of the tale is researched and legally accurate. This story describes the events of a criminal prosecution as they would actually unfold; nothing is made up or embellished. Legal terms, where they are used, can be looked up in the glossary.
http://tqd.advanced.org/2760/homep.htm

THEELECTRICCHAIR.COM

The author of this site hoped to create a web version of a short film he made about his visit to New York State's electric chair. For this site he expanded his focus to include the death penalty in general. The site contains articles, photos, and even videos of all the various ways throughout history to execute somebody. Some of the material is graphic and should be viewed with caution.
http://www.theelectricchair.com/index.htm

PRODEATHPENALTY.COM

This site was developed as a resource for those searching the internet for pro-death-penalty information and resources. The authors note that capital punishment is a topic that brings up deep emotional reactions. Those searching the internet are likely to find thousands of websites related to the topic. With very few exceptions, these sites are anti-death-penalty. People who are adamantly opposed to the death penalty tend to take an activist stance and become involved in working to stop the death penalty. For the most part, people who support the death penalty do so quietly, more in their own minds than in any public fashion. The site plans to include a database of the victims of death row inmates.
http://www.prodeathpenalty.com

THE CLARK COUNTY PROSECUTING ATTORNEY—DEATH PENALTY LINKS

This site, produced by the prosecuting attorney of Clark County in Indiana, contains more than one thousand death penalty links. If you need a starting point for research this may be all you need.
http://www.clarkprosecutor.org/html/links/dplinks.htm

SELECTED ARTICLES ON THE DEATH PENALTY

This is an anti-death-penalty site, with dozens of links to issues, articles, and state-specific information. This site is very useful for anyone seeking original anti-death-penalty articles.
http://d.witmer.tripod.com/Death_Penalty.html

DERECHOS HUMAN RIGHTS—DEATH PENALTY LINKS

This organization works against violations of human rights and humanitarian law all over the world. They believe the death penalty is a human rights issue. The site provides a well-organized list of resources on the death penalty.
http://www.derechos.org/dp

Is It Time to Give Up the War on Drugs?

The Office of National Drug Control Policy (ONDCP), which oversees virtually all U.S. anti-drug efforts, recently released its annual report on *The National Drug Control Strategy, 1999*. The study states that 13.9 million Americans over the age of 12 are "current" drug users and that "34.8 percent of Americans 12 and older have used an illegal drug in their lifetime." The report also notes that a survey conducted by the Columbia University Center for Addiction and Substance Abuse found that "41 percent of teens had attended parties where marijuana was available, and 30 percent had seen drugs sold at school." The continued availability and use of illegal drugs within our society remains a disturbing reality.

Over the past ten years, the federal government has spent more than $150 billion to fight drugs. What have we received for our investment? Some think it's not much. In the name of fighting drugs, the United States has dispatched troops to Bolivia, built a paramilitary base in Peru, eradicated crops in Colombia, sent AWACS spy planes over the Caribbean, installed X-ray machines along the Mexican border, erected an electronic curtain around South Florida, and invaded Panama. It has dismantled the Medellín and Cali cartels, the two great Colombian cocaine syndicates said to control the flow of drugs into the United States. Despite it all, the cocaine market continues to exist, and heroin is readily available at record high rates of purity. And, while the number of casual drug users has decreased, the number of hardcore, addicted users has not.

Progress toward ending the drug war, however, continues to run into one major obstacle: the lack of a clear alternative. If we are to end the war on drugs, what should take its place? The most frequent answer is legalization. If the drug war is failing, then legalizing drugs is presented as the only alternative. On the surface, the idea of legalization has appeal. If drugs were legalized, the whole noxious network of drug traffickers, smugglers, and money launderers stretching from the jungles of South America to the streets of our inner cities would suddenly disappear. Law enforcement efforts could be redirected against other types of crime.

Yet legalization entails some risks. If hard drugs like heroin or crack were suddenly sold in state stores or made available through prescription, use—and abuse—could increase. The end of Prohibition, for instance, resulted in a sharp rise in alcohol consumption, along with many unfortunate side effects. And, while no one wants to revive that disastrous experiment, it does suggest that the sudden legalization of an intoxicant can lead to a spurt in consumption. It is this prospect that keeps many Americans from endorsing the idea of legalizing drugs—or at least hard ones.

Joshua Wolf Shenk, in "Why You Can Hate Drugs and Still Want to Legalize Them," believes we are caught between the horror of drug abuse and the horror of the illegal drug trade. Making drugs legally available, with tight regulatory controls, would end the black market and with it much of the violence, crime, and drug-related social pathology. Yet, history shows that lifting prohibition would most likely produce more drug use, and more abuse and addiction. We are presented with a choice between two difficult options. But Shenk believes that drug prohibition does more harm than good and that legalization is the best alternative.

James A. Inciardi and Christine A. Saum disagree and, in "Legalization Madness," claim that with legalization, the overall rate of violent crime would increase. They say that legalizing drugs would also increase physical illnesses and compound any existing psychiatric problems among users and their family members. Nor would legalizing drugs eliminate the effects of unemployment, inadequate housing, deficient job skills, economic worries, and physical abuse that typically contribute to the use of drugs.

Yes

Why You Can Hate Drugs and Still Want to Legalize Them

Joshua
Wolf Shenk

There's no breeze, only bare, stifling heat, but Kevin can scarcely support his wispy frame. He bobs forward, his eyes slowly closing until he drifts asleep, in a 45-degree hunch. "Kevin?" I say softly. He jerks awake and slowly rubs a hand over his spindly chest. "It's so hot in here I can hardly think," he says.

. . .

This July, I spent a long, hot day talking to junkies in New York City, in a run-down hotel near Columbia University. Some, like Kevin, were reticent. Others spoke freely about their lives and addictions. I sat with Melissa for 20 minutes as she patiently hunted her needle-scarred legs for a vein to take a spike. She had just fixed after a long dry spell. "I was sick," she told me. "I could hardly move. And Papo"—she gestures toward a friend sitting across from her—"he helped me out. He gave me something to make me better."

To most Americans, addicts like Kevin and Melissa and Papo are not people, but arguments. Some victims of drug use inspire sympathy, or irritation, or just plain worry. But it is the junkies—seemingly bereft of humanity, subsisting in what one former addict calls "soul-death"—who justify our national attitude toward certain drugs: that they should be illegal, unavailable, and totally suppressed.

. . .

Addicts suffer from illegal drugs. But each year hundreds of children … are killed because drugs are illegal. It's difficult, but crucial, to understand this distinction. By turning popular drugs into illegal contraband, prohibition sparks tremendous inflation. Small amounts of plant leaves and powder that

From *The Washington Monthly* (October 1995). Copyright © 1995 by The Washington Monthly, Washington, D.C. Reprinted with the permission of the publishers.

cost only pennies to grow and process sell for hundreds of dollars on the street. All told, the black market in this country takes in $50 to $60 billion in income each year. In lawful society, such a large industry would be regulated by rules and enforcement mechanisms. But the intense competition of the black market is regulated only by violence. Rival entrepreneurs don't go to the courts with a dispute. They shoot it out in the street.

The black market now holds entire communities in its grip. In addition to the violence—and crime driven by addicts supporting expensive habits—the fast cash of dealing lures many young people away from school, into the drug trade, and often onto a track toward jail or death.

We are caught, then, between the ... horror of drug abuse and the horror of the illegal drug trade. Making drugs legally available, with tight regulatory controls, would end the black market, and with it much of the violence, crime, and social pathology we have come to understand as "drug-related." And yet, history shows clearly that lifting prohibition would allow for more drug use, and more abuse and addiction.

...

The choice between two intensely unpleasant options is never easy. But, considering this problem in all its depth and complexity, it becomes clear that drug prohibition does more harm than good. We can't discount the problem of drug abuse (and that includes the abuse of legal drugs). But prohibition didn't keep Kevin from becoming an addict in the first place, and it certainly isn't helping him stop. High prices for drugs do discourage some would-be users, though far fewer than the government would like. The fact is we have done a very poor job discouraging drug use with the blunt force of law. The hundreds of billions of dollars spent on drug control in the last several decades have yielded only a moderate decline in the casual use of marijuana and cocaine. But there has been no decrease in hard-core addiction. The total amount of cocaine consumed per capita has actually risen. And even casual use is now creeping up.

Government does have a responsibility to limit the individual and social costs of drug use, but such efforts must be balanced against the harm they cause. And ending the drug war needn't mean a surrender to addiction, or an affirmation of reckless drug use. President Clinton's stance on cigarette addiction—that cigarettes can be both legal and tightly regulated, particularly with respect to advertising aimed at children—points to a middle ground. Potentially, we could do a better job of fighting drug abuse, while avoiding the vicious side-effects of an outright ban.

Comparing the Costs

Unfortunately, this country's discussion of "the drug problem" is marked by little clear analysis and much misinformation. Politicians and bureaucrats minimize or entirely ignore the consequences of prohibition. At the other

extreme, libertarians call for government to withdraw from regulating intoxicants entirely.

···

In communities where two-thirds of the youth lack the schooling or
skills to get a decent job, drug dealing is both lucrative and glamorous. Rich
dealers are role models and images of entrepreneurial success—the Bill
Gateses of the inner city. Unlike straight jobs, though, dealing drugs means
entering a world of gruesome violence.

···

Although it is popular these days to blame welfare for undermining the
work ethic, often overlooked is the role played by the black market's twist-
ed incentives, which lure men away from school and legitimate work—
and, often, away from their families.

···

A Nation behind Bars

The high prices caused by prohibition drive crime in another way: Addicts
need cash to feed their habits. The junkies I met in New York told me they
would spend between $200 and $600 a week for drugs. Melissa, for example, once had a good job and made enough to pay her bills and to buy dope.
Then she got laid off and turned to prostitution to support her habit. Others steal to pay for their drugs—from liquor stores, from their families, from
dealers, or from other addicts. According to a study by the Bureau of Justice Statistics, one out of every three thefts are committed by people seeking drug money.

This crime wave does not restrict itself to the inner cities. Addicts seeking money to get a fix are very fond of the fine appliances and cash-filled
wallets found in wealthier neighborhoods. Suburban high schools may not
have swarms of dealers crawling through the fences, but dealers are there,
too. In fact, the suburbs are increasingly popular for dealers looking to take
up residence.

Quite apart from the costs of the black market—the crime, the neighborhoods and lives ruined—Americans also pay a heavy price for the drug
war itself. For fiscal 1996, Clinton has requested $14.6 billion for drug con-
trol (up from only $1.3 billion in 1983). State and local governments spend
about twice that each year.

But these budgets reflect only a small portion of the costs. In 1980, the
United States had 330,000 people in jail; today, it's well over a million, and
drug offenders account for 46 percent of that increase. On top of the cost
of building prisons, it takes more than $30,000 per year to keep someone
in jail. Naturally, prison spending has exploded. The country now spends
nearly $30 billion annually on corrections. Between 1970 and 1990, state
and local governments hiked prison spending by 232 percent.

Even worse, thanks to mandatory minimum sentences, the system is overloaded with non-violent drug users and dealers, who now often receive harsher penalties than murderers, rapists, and serious white-collar criminals.... Non-violent drug offenders receive an average 60 months in jail time, five times the average 12-month sentence for manslaughter convicts.

Some people may say: Build more jails. In an era of tax cuts and fiscal freezes, though, every dollar spent on corrections comes from roads, or health care, or education. Even with the huge growth in prison spending, three-fourths of all state prisons were operating over their maximum capacity in 1992. Even conservatives like Michael Quinlan, director of the Federal Bureau of Prisons under Reagan and Bush, have had enough of this insanity. "They're locking up a lot of people who are not serious or violent offenders," he says. "That ... brings serious consequences in terms of our ability to incarcerate truly violent criminals."

If sticking a drug dealer in jail meant fewer dealers on the street, perhaps this wave of incarceration would eventually do some good. But it doesn't work like that: Lock up a murderer, and you have one less murderer on the street. Lock up a dealer, and you create a job opening. It's like jailing an IBM executive; the pay is good, the job is appealing, so someone will move into the office before long. Clearing dealers from one neighborhood only means they'll move to another. Busting a drug ring only makes room for a competitor.

...

Illegal drugs, left unregulated, are also much more dangerous than they need to be. Imagine drinking whisky with no idea of its potency.... Virtually all "overdose" deaths from the use of illegal drugs are due to contaminants or the user's ignorance of the drug's potency. "Just deserts," one might say. But isn't the basis of our drug policy supposed to be concern for people's health and well-being?

...

Given the terrible consequences of drug abuse, any reasonable person is bound to object: How could we even consider making drugs generally available? But have you asked why alcohol and tobacco are kept generally available?

Tobacco products—linked to cancer of the lungs, throat, larynx, and ovaries—cause 30 percent of all cancer deaths. Even more tobacco-related deaths come from heart attacks and strokes. Every year 435,000 Americans suffer premature deaths because of cigarettes. And, of course, nicotine is extremely addictive: The Surgeon General has found that the "capture" rate—the percentage of people who become addicted after trying it—is higher with cigarettes than any other drug, legal or illegal. Most nicotine addicts are hooked before age 18.

Alcohol is even more destructive. Extensive drinking often results in bleeding ulcers, cirrhosis of the liver, stomach and intestinal inflammation, and muscle damage, as well as severe damage to the brain and nervous system, manifested by blackouts and psychotic episodes.

As for social costs, alcohol is the most likely of all mind-altering substances to induce criminal behavior, according to the National Institute of Justice. Close to 11 million Americans are alcoholics, and another 7 million are alcohol abusers—meaning they've screwed up at work, been in an accident, or been arrested because of drinking. Drunk driving is the cause of a third of all traffic fatalities. Alcohol-related problems affect one out of every four American homes, and alcoholism is involved in 60 percent of all murders and 38 percent of child abuse cases. These statistics only confirm our everyday experience. Who doesn't know of a family shattered by an alcoholic, or someone who has suffered with an alcoholic boss?

The reason that alcohol and tobacco are legal, despite the damage they do, is that prohibition would be even worse. In the case of alcohol, we know from experience. The prohibition from 1919 to 1933 is now synonymous with violence, organized crime, and corruption. Financed by huge profits from bootlegging, gangsters like Al Capone terrorized cities and eluded the best efforts of law enforcement. It soon became too much.

After prohibition's repeal, consumption rates for alcohol did in fact rise. But as anyone who was alive in 1933 could tell you, the increase was hardly an explosion. And it seems likely that the rise was fueled by advertising and the movies.

...

What we have had a hard time learning is that there are a plethora of options between prohibition and laissez-faire. In 1933, after prohibition, the federal government withdrew entirely from regulating the market in spirits. No limits were placed on marketing or advertising, and the siege from Madison Avenue and Hollywood began immediately. For years, the government seemed unable to counter the excesses of legal drug pushers like Philip Morris and Seagrams. Ads for tobacco, beer, and liquor dominated the worlds of art and entertainment.

The tide began to turn in 1964, when the Surgeon General issued the first of a series of reports on the dangers of smoking. In 1971 cigarette ads were banned from TV and radio. The media began to open its eyes as well. Meanwhile, there was an equally important change in attitudes. It was once respectable to drink two or three martinis at a business lunch. Today it is not. Nor do we wink at drunk driving or smoking by pregnant women. Cigarette use, in fact, has declined dramatically since the sixties.

But much has been left undone. The TV and radio ban, for example, left the bulk of cigarette marketing untouched. And ironically, tobacco companies didn't much mind the ban, because it also dealt a severe blow to a campaign of negative advertising. Under the "fairness doctrine," TV and radio stations in the late sixties gave free air time to anti-smoking spots, such as one that mocked the Marlboro man by showing him coughing and wheezing. These ads were extremely effective, more so, many believed, than the Surgeon General's warnings. Once the tobacco ads were banned, though, TV and radio stations were no longer required to run the negative spots.

It is high time to begin a massive campaign of negative advertising against both cigarettes and alcohol. And we can ban advertising for intoxicants entirely.

...

The same approach should be employed with now-illegal drugs. An end to prohibition need not mean official endorsement of crack or heroin, but instead could be an opportunity to redouble efforts to limit their use. Drug use would rise after prohibition—but it wouldn't be the catastrophic explosion that drug warriors predict. They count on both distortions of history (claiming an explosion of alcohol use in 1933) and exaggerations of the dangers of cocaine, heroin, and speed—not to mention marijuana and hallucinogens. Though all intoxicants should be taken seriously, these drugs are neither as powerful, addictive, or attractive as many imagine. Among the population of nonusers, 97 percent of Americans say they would be "not very likely" or "not at all likely" to try cocaine if it were legal. And even those who would try it in a legal regime would not find themselves immediately in the grip of an insatiable habit. As with alcohol, heavy dependence on cocaine and heroin is acquired over time.

...

Of course, lifting prohibition would not be a panacea for our most troubled communities. But imagine the benefits of cutting out the black market. Profit would be eliminated from the drug trade, which means kids wouldn't be drawn to dealing, addicts wouldn't be pushed to thieving, and the sea of violence and crime would ebb.

...

Meanwhile, police could focus on real crime—and they'd have the prison space to lock up violent or repeat offenders. Businesses, now scared off by inner-city crime, might be drawn back into these communities, and a cycle of recovery could begin. For drug addicts, the federal government could spend the billions now wasted on law enforcement and interdiction to provide effective treatment.

At the same time, the government could clamp down on the alcohol and cigarette corporate behemoths, and make sure that they never get their hands on now-illegal drugs by controlling distribution through package stores—displaying warnings in the stores and on containers themselves. Advertising and marketing, clearly, would be prohibited and government would also have to fund an intensive campaign of public education to prevent misuse, abuse, and addiction.

Beyond government, we must recognize as a culture the damage done by drugs—even if we accept the rights of individuals to use them. The entertainment industry should take this responsibility very seriously. As it is, the scare tactics used by the government give even greater currency to Hollywood's images of the hip, outlaw drug user.

After so many years of prohibition—and a vociferous government effort to distort the truth—it's not hard to imagine why people would fear an epidemic of new drug addicts after prohibition. But such fears are exaggerated. The increase in use could be kept to a minimum by smart public policy. Meanwhile, we would be undoing the horror of present policy—which fractures communities, leaves kids scared to go to the playground, and pushes young men toward death or jail.

With reforms, we could stop this great damage. The good, almost certainly, would far overshadow the new problems created. Isn't it a moral imperative that we at least try? If legalization proves to be a failure—though the best evidence indicates it would not—we could return to present policy, or find a third way.

Many may be tempted to split the difference—maintain prohibition, but ease some of the penalties. Or legalize the mildest of the illegal drugs, such as marijuana. Or make drugs available to addicts by prescription. There's nothing to prevent experimenting with different strategies. But remember, the tighter the restrictions, the more fuel to the fire of the black market. Undermining the black market has to be the principle of any reform. The other temptation is to justify the costs of prohibition in moral terms—"drugs are evil." But pining for a "drug-free America" doesn't change the reality that we'll never have one. Even Lee Brown concedes that the best he can do—with a budget approaching $15 billion dollars—is reduce drug use by 5 percent annually. Is dissuading a few hundred thousand marijuana users worth the terror of the black market?

Ultimately drug policy does come down to tradeoffs. The simple truth is that humans are tempted by intoxicants. And, in a free society like ours, the rights of life and liberty will always be accompanied by people pursuing stiff drinks, or lines of cocaine, or marijuana cigarettes. Inflating the price of drugs through prohibition and jailing sellers and users of drugs sprang from a noble sentiment—that we could eliminate the scourge of addiction, or limit it significantly. Now we know that the enormous efforts in law enforcement have yielded few benefits in curbing drug abuse—and are a paltry disincentive for many drug users and would-be users. The prohibition experiment has failed. The time has come to recognize the great harm it has done. The United States is now akin to a person with poison ivy, scratching furiously at the rashes, and holding fast in denial when they do not go away: Soon, the blood begins to flow. These wounds show themselves every day, in brutal murders and bleak urban landscapes.

We will always have a "drug problem" of some sort. The question is: What kind of drug problem? Ultimately, choosing between regulation and prohibition turns on a simple question: Is it better to allow some individuals to make a bad choice, or to subject many, many innocent people to drive-by shootings, rampant crime, and dangerous schools? The moral policy is to protect the innocent—and then do our best to help the others as well.

Legalization Madness

James A.
Inciardi and
Christine A. Saum

Frustrated by the government's apparent inability to reduce the supply of illegal drugs on the streets of America, and disquieted by media accounts of innocents victimized by drug-related violence, some policymakers are convinced that the "war on drugs" has failed. In an attempt to find a better solution to the "drug crisis" or, at the very least, to try an alternative strategy, they have proposed legalizing drugs.

They argue that, if marijuana, cocaine, heroin, and other drugs were legalized, several positive things would probably occur: (1) Drug prices would fall; (2) users would obtain their drugs at low, government-regulated prices, and they would no longer be forced to resort to crime in order to support their habits; (3) levels of drug-related crime, and particularly violent crime, would significantly decline, resulting in less crowded courts, jails, and prisons (this would allow law-enforcement personnel to focus their energies on the "real criminals" in society); and (4) the drug production, distribution, and sale would no longer be controlled by organized crime, and thus such criminal syndicates as the Colombian cocaine "cartels," the Jamaican "posses," and the various "mafias" around the country and the world would be decapitalized, and the violence associated with drug distribution rivalries would be eliminated.

By contrast, the anti-legalization camp argues that violent crime would not necessarily decline in a legalized drug market. In fact, there are three reasons why it might actually increase. First, removing the criminal sanctions against the possession and distribution of illegal drugs would make them more available and attractive and, hence, would create large numbers of new users. Second, an increase in use would lead to a greater number of

From *The Public Interest* (March 22, 1996). Copyright © 1996 by National Affairs, Inc. Reprinted with the permission of *The Public Interest*. All rights reserved.

dysfunctional addicts who could not support themselves, their habits, or their lifestyles through legitimate means. Hence crime would be their only alternative. Third, more users would mean more of the violence associated with the ingestion of drugs.

These divergent points of view tend to persist because the relationships between drugs and crime are quite complex and because the possible outcomes of a legalized drug market are based primarily on speculation. However, it is possible, from a careful review of the existing empirical literature on drugs and violence, to make some educated inferences.

Considering "Legalization"

Yet much depends upon what we mean by "legalizing drugs." Would all currently illicit drugs be legalized or would the experiment be limited to just certain ones? True legalization would be akin to selling such drugs as heroin and cocaine on the open market, much like alcohol and tobacco, with a few age-related restrictions. In contrast, there are "medicalization" and "decriminalization" alternatives. Medicalization approaches are of many types, but, in essence, they would allow users to obtain prescriptions for some, or all, currently illegal substances. Decriminalization removes the criminal penalties associated with the possession of small amounts of illegal drugs for personal use, while leaving intact the sanctions for trafficking, distribution, and sale.

But what about crack-cocaine? A quick review of the literature reveals that the legalizers, the decriminalizers, and the medicalizers avoid talking about this particular form of cocaine. Perhaps they do not want to legalize crack out of fear of the drug itself, or of public outrage.

...

There is a related concern associated with the legalization of cocaine. Because crack is easily manufactured from powder cocaine ... many drug-policy reformers hold that no form of cocaine should be legalized. But this weakens the argument that legalization will reduce drug-related violence, for much of this violence would appear to be in the cocaine-and-crack-distribution markets.

To better understand the complex relationship between drugs and violence, we will discuss the data in the context of three models developed by Paul J. Goldstein of the University of Illinois at Chicago. They are the "psychopharmacological," "economically compulsive," and "systemic" explanations of violence. The first model holds, correctly in our view, that some individuals may become excitable, irrational, and even violent due to the ingestion of specific drugs. In contrast, taking a more economic approach to the behavior of drug users, the second holds that some drug users engage in violent crime mainly for the sake of supporting their drug use. The third model maintains that drug-related violent crime is simply the result of the drug market under a regime of illegality.

Psychopharmacological Violence

The case for legalization rests in part upon the faulty assumption that drugs themselves do not cause violence; rather, so goes the argument, violence is the result of depriving drug addicts of drugs or of the "criminal" trafficking in drugs. But, as researcher Barry Spunt points out, "Users of drugs do get violent when they get high."

Research has documented that chronic users of amphetamines, methamphetamine, and cocaine in particular tend to exhibit hostile and aggressive behaviors. Psychopharmacological violence can also be a product of what is known as "cocaine psychosis." As dose and duration of cocaine use increase, the development of cocaine-related psychopathology is not uncommon. Cocaine psychosis is generally preceded by a transitional period characterized by increased suspiciousness, compulsive behavior, fault finding, and eventually paranoia. When the psychotic state is reached, individuals may experience visual, as well as auditory, hallucinations, with persecutory voices commonly heard. Many believe that they are being followed by police or that family, friends, and others are plotting against them.

Moreover, everyday events are sometimes misinterpreted by cocaine users in ways that support delusional beliefs. When coupled with the irritability and hyperactivity that cocaine tends to generate in almost all of its users, the cocaine-induced paranoia may lead to violent behavior as a means of "self-defense" against imagined persecutors. The violence associated with cocaine psychosis is a common feature in many crack houses across the United States. Violence may also result from the irritability associated with drug-withdrawal syndromes. In addition, some users ingest drugs before committing crimes to both loosen inhibitions and bolster their resolve to break the law.

Acts of violence may result from either periodic or chronic use of a drug. For example, in a study of drug use and psychopathy among Baltimore City jail inmates, researchers at the University of Baltimore reported that cocaine use was related to irritability, resentment, hostility, and assault. They concluded that these indicators of aggression may be a function of drug effects rather than of a predisposition to these behaviors. Similarly, Barry Spunt and his colleagues at National Development and Research Institutes (NDRI) in New York City found that of 269 convicted murderers incarcerated in New York State prisons, 45 percent were high at the time of the offense. Three in ten believed that the homicide was related to their drug use, challenging conventional beliefs that violence only infrequently occurs as a result of drug consumption.

Even marijuana, which pro-legalizers consider harmless, may have a connection with violence and crime. Spunt and his colleagues attempted to determine the role of marijuana in the crimes of the homicide offenders they interviewed in the New York State prisons. One-third of those who had ever used marijuana had smoked the drug in the 24-hour period prior to the homicide. Moreover, 31 percent of those who considered themselves to be "high" at the time of committing murder felt that the homicide and marijuana were related. William Blount of the University of South Florida interviewed abused women in prisons and shelters for battered women located throughout Florida. He and his colleagues found that 24 percent of those who killed their abusers were marijuana users while only 8 percent of those who did not kill their abusers smoked marijuana.

Alcohol Abuse

A point that needs emphasizing is that alcohol, because it is legal, accessible, and inexpensive, is linked to violence to a far greater extent than any illegal drug. For example, in the study just cited, it was found that an impressive 64 percent of those women who eventually killed their abusers were alcohol users (44 percent of those who did not kill their abusers were alcohol users). Indeed, the extent to which alcohol is responsible for violent crimes in comparison with other drugs is apparent from the statistics. For example, Carolyn Block and her colleagues at the Criminal Justice Information Authority in Chicago found that, between 1982 and 1989, the use of alcohol by offenders or victims in local homicides ranged from 18 percent to 32 percent.

Alcohol has, in fact, been consistently linked to homicide. Spunt and his colleagues interviewed 268 homicide offenders incarcerated in New York State correctional facilities to determine the role of alcohol in their crimes: Thirty-one percent of the respondents reported being drunk at the time of the crime and 19 percent believed that the homicide was related to their drinking. More generally, Douglass Murdoch of Quebec's McGill University found that in some 9,000 criminal cases drawn from a multinational sample, 62 percent of violent offenders were drinking shortly before, or at the time of, the offense.

It appears that alcohol reduces the inhibitory control of threat, making it more likely that a person will exhibit violent behaviors normally suppressed by fear. In turn, this reduction of inhibition heightens the probability that intoxicated persons will perpetrate, or become victims of, aggressive behavior.

When analyzing the psychopharmacological model of drugs and violence, most of the discussions focus on the offender and the role of drugs in causing or facilitating crime. But what about the victims? Are the victims of drug- and alcohol-related homicides simply casualties of someone else's substance abuse? In addressing these questions, the data demonstrates that victims are likely to be drug users as well. For example, in an analysis of the 4,298 homicides that occurred in New York City during 1990 and 1991, Kenneth Tardiff of Cornell University Medical College found that the victims of these offenses were 10 to 50 times more likely to be cocaine users than were members of the general population. Of the white female victims, 60 percent in the 25- to 34-year age group had cocaine in their systems—

for black females, the figure was 72 percent. Tardiff speculated that the classic symptoms of cocaine use—irritability, paranoia, aggressiveness—may have instigated the violence. In another study of cocaine users in New York City, female high-volume users were found to be victims of violence far more frequently than low-volume and nonusers of cocaine. Studies in numerous other cities and countries have yielded the same general findings—that a great many of the victims of homicide and other forms of violence are drinkers and drug users themselves.

Economically Compulsive Violence

Supporters of the economically compulsive model of violence argue that in a legalized market, the prices of "expensive drugs" would decline to more affordable levels, and, hence, predatory crimes would become unnecessary. This argument is based on several specious assumptions. First, it assumes that there is empirical support for what has been referred to as the "enslavement theory of addiction." Second, it assumes that people addicted to drugs commit crimes only for the purpose of supporting their habits. Third, it assumes that, in a legalized market, users could obtain as much of the drugs as they wanted whenever they wanted. Finally, it assumes that, if drugs are inexpensive, they will be affordable, and thus crime would be unnecessary.

With respect to the first premise, there has been for the better part of this century a concerted belief among many in the drug-policy field that addicts commit crimes because they are "enslaved" to drugs, and further that, because of the high price of heroin, cocaine, and other illicit chemicals on the black market, users are forced to commit crimes in order to support their drug habits. However, there is no solid empirical evidence to support this contention. From the 1920s through the end of the 1960s, hundreds of studies of the relationship between crime and addiction were conducted. Invariably, when one analysis would support the posture of "enslavement theory," the next would affirm the view that addicts were criminals first and that their drug use was but one more manifestation of their deviant lifestyles. In retrospect, the difficulty lay in the ways that many of the studies had been conducted: Biases and deficiencies in research designs and sampling had rendered their findings of little value.

Studies since the mid-1970s of active drug users on the streets of New York, Miami, Baltimore, and elsewhere have demonstrated that the "enslavement theory" has little basis in reality. All of these studies of the criminal careers of drug users have convincingly documented that, while drug use tends to intensify and perpetuate criminal behavior, it usually does not initiate criminal careers. In fact, the evidence suggests that among the majority of street drug users who are involved in crime, their criminal careers are well-established prior to the onset of either narcotics or cocaine use. As such, it would appear that the "inference of causality"—that the high price of drugs on the black market itself causes crime—is simply false.

Looking at the second premise, a variety of studies show that addicts commit crimes for reasons other than supporting their drug habit. They do so also for daily living expenses. For example, researchers at the Center for Drug and Alcohol Studies at the University of Delaware who studied crack users on the streets of Miami found that, of the active addicts interviewed, 85 percent of the male and 70 percent of the female interviewees paid for portions of their living expenses through street crime. In fact, one-half of the men and one-fourth of the women paid for 90 percent or more of their living expenses through crime. And, not surprisingly, 96 percent of the men and 99 percent of the women had not held a legal job in the 90-day period before being interviewed for the study.

With respect to the third premise, that in a legalized market users could obtain as much of the drugs as they wanted whenever they wanted, only speculation is possible. More than likely, however, there would be some sort of regulation, and hence black markets for drugs would persist for those whose addictions were beyond the medicalized or legalized allotments. In a decriminalized market, levels of drug-related violence would likely either remain unchanged or increase (if drug use increased).

As for the last premise, that cheap drugs preclude the need to commit crimes to obtain them, the evidence emphatically suggests that this is not the case. Consider crack-cocaine: Although crack "rocks" are available on the illegal market for as little as two dollars in some locales, users are still involved in crime-driven endeavors to support their addictions. For example, researchers Norman S. Miller and Mark S. Gold surveyed 200 consecutive callers to the 1-800-COCAINE hotline who considered themselves to have a problem with crack. They found that, despite the low cost of crack, 63 percent of daily users and 40 percent of non-daily users spent more than $200 per week on the drug. Similarly, interviews conducted by NDRI researchers in New York City with almost 1,000 drug users contacted in the streets, jails, and treatment programs revealed that almost one-half of them spent over $1,000 a month on crack. The study also documented that crack users—despite the low cost of their drug of choice—spent more money on drugs than did users of heroin, powder cocaine, marijuana, and alcohol.

Systemic Violence

It is the supposed systemic violence associated with trafficking in cocaine and crack in America's inner cities that has recently received the attention of drug-policy critics interested in legalizing drugs. Certainly it might appear that, if heroin and cocaine were legal substances, systemic drug-related violence would decline. However, there are two very important questions in this regard: First, is drug-related violence more often psychopharmacological or systemic? Second, is the great bulk of systemic violence related to the distribution of crack? If most of the drug-related violence is psychopharmacological in nature, and if systemic violence is typically related to crack—the drug generally excluded from consideration when legalization is recommended—then legalizing drugs would probably not reduce violent crime.

Regarding the first question, several recent studies conducted in New York City tend to contradict, or at least not support, the notion that legalizing drugs would reduce violent, systemic-related crime. For example, Paul J. Goldstein's ethnographic studies of male and female drug users during the late 1980s found that cocaine-related violence was more often psychopharmacological than systemic. Similarly, Kenneth Tardiff's study of 4,298 New York City homicides found that 31 percent of the victims had used cocaine in the 24-hour period prior to their deaths. One of the conclusions of the study was that the homicides were not necessarily related to drug dealing. In all likelihood, as victims of homicide, the cocaine users may have provoked violence through their irritability, paranoid thinking, and verbal or physical aggression—all of which are among the psychopharmacological effects of cocaine.

Regarding the second question, the illegal drug most associated with systemic violence is crack-cocaine. Of all illicit drugs, crack is the one now responsible for the most homicides. In a study done in New York City in 1988 by Goldstein and his colleagues, crack was found to be connected with 32 percent of all homicides and 60 percent of all drug-related homicides. Furthermore, although there is evidence that crack sellers are more violent than other drug sellers, this violence is not confined to the drug-selling context—violence potentials appear to precede involvement in selling.... If this is the case, does anyone really believe that we can improve these complex social problems through the simple act of legalizing drugs?

Don't Just Say No

The issue of whether or not legalization would create a multitude of new users also needs to be addressed. It has been shown that many people do not use drugs simply because drugs are illegal.

...

Although there is no way of accurately estimating how many new users there would be if drugs were legalized, there would probably be many. To begin with, there is the historical example of Prohibition. During Prohibition, there was a decrease of 20 percent to 50 percent in the number of alcoholics. These estimates were calculated based on a decline in cirrhosis and other alcohol-related deaths; after Prohibition ended, both of these indicators increased.

Currently, relatively few people are steady users of drugs. The University of Michigan's Monitoring the Future study reported in 1995 that only two-tenths of 1 percent of high-school seniors are daily users of either hallucinogens, cocaine, heroin, sedatives, or inhalants. It is the addicts who overwhelmingly consume the bulk of the drug supply—80 percent of all alcohol and almost 100 percent of all heroin. In other words, there are significantly large numbers of non-users who have yet to even try drugs, let alone use them regularly. Of those who begin to use drugs "recreationally," researchers estimate that approximately 10 percent go on to serious, heavy, chronic, compulsive use. Herbert Kleber, the former deputy director of the Office of National Drug Control Policy, recently estimated that cocaine legalization might multiply the number of addicts from the current 2 million to between 18 and 50 million (which are the estimated numbers of problem drinkers and nicotine addicts).

This suggests that drug prohibition seems to be having some very positive effects and that legalizing drugs would not necessarily have a depressant effect on violent crime. With legalization, violent crime would likely escalate; or perhaps some types of systemic violence would decline at the expense of greatly increasing the overall rate of violent crime. Moreover, legalizing drugs would likely increase physical illnesses and compound any existing psychiatric problems among users and their family members. And finally, legalizing drugs would not eliminate the effects of unemployment, inadequate housing, deficient job skills, economic worries, and physical abuse that typically contribute to the use of drugs.

KEY WEBSITES

BUREAU OF JUSTICE STATISTICS—DRUGS AND CRIME FACTS

This site summarizes U.S. statistics about drug-related crimes, law enforcement, courts, and corrections from Bureau of Justice Statistics (BJS) and non-BJS sources. It updates the information published in *Drugs and Crime Facts*, and will be revised as new information becomes available. The data provide policymakers, criminal justice practitioners, researchers, and the general public with online access to understandable information on various drug law violations and drug-related law enforcement.

http://www.ojp.usdoj.gov/bjs/dcf/contents.htm

THE LINDESMITH CENTER

The Lindesmith Center is a policy research institute that focuses on broadening the debate on drug policy and related issues. The center houses a library and information center, acts as a link between scholars, government, and the media, and undertakes projects on special topics such as methadone policy reform and alternatives to drug testing in the workplace. The guiding principle of the center is harm reduction, an alternative approach to drug policy, and treatment that focuses on minimizing the adverse effects of both drug use and drug prohibition. Particular attention is focused on analyzing the experiences of foreign countries in reducing drug-related harms.

http://www.lindesmith.org

NIDA, NATIONAL INSTITUTE OF DRUG ABUSE

NIDA is part of the National Institutes of Health, Department of Health and Human Services. The Institute plays an important role in programs of drug abuse research. NIDA hopes to further understanding of how drugs of abuse affect the brain and behavior. It is also working to ensure the rapid and effective transfer of scientific data to policymakers, drug abuse practitioners, other health care practitioners, and the general public. The scientific knowledge that is generated through NIDA research is a critical element to improving the overall health of the nation. NIDA's goal is to ensure that science, not ideology or anecdote, forms the foundation for U.S. drug abuse reduction efforts.

http://www.nida.nih.gov/NIDAHome1.html

NATIONAL CLEARINGHOUSE FOR DRUG AND ALCOHOL INFORMATION

The National Clearinghouse for Alcohol and Drug Information (NCADI) is the information service of the Center for Substance Abuse Prevention of the U.S. Department of Health and Human Services. NCADI is the world's largest resource for current information and materials about alcohol and other drugs.

http://www.health.org

THE DRUG POLICY FOUNDATION

The Drug Policy Foundation is an independent, nonprofit organization representing over 24,000 individuals who favor alternatives to the current war on drugs. The group believes that current drug policy is not working and that it is time to examine reasoned and compassionate alternatives. The Drug Policy Foundation favors a shift away from criminal justice policies and a shift toward public health approaches to drug use and abuse.
http://www.dpf.org

THE NATIONAL CENTER ON ADDICTION
AND SUBSTANCE ABUSE AT COLUMBIA UNIVERSITY

The goal of the Center is to (1) inform Americans of the economic and social costs of substance abuse and its impact on their lives; (2) assess what works in prevention, treatment, and law enforcement; (3) encourage every individual and institution to take responsibility to combat substance abuse and addiction; (4) provide those on the front lines with the tools they need to succeed; (5) remove the stigma of abuse and replace shame and despair with hope.
http://www.casacolumbia.org

COMMON SENSE FOR DRUG POLICY

Common Sense for Drug Policy is a nonprofit organization dedicated to expanding discussion on drug policy through questioning our existing laws and educating the public about alternatives to current policies.
http://www.csdp.org

ACLU DRUG POLICY

The American Civil Liberties Union Freedom Network believes the best way to deal with drugs is through regulation. The ACLU opposes criminal prohibition, not only because of the current policy's failure to deal effectively with the drug problem, but also because it subjects otherwise law-abiding citizens to arrest, prosecution, and imprisonment.
http://www.aclu.org/issues/drugpolicy/hmdrugpolicy.html

NATIONAL ORGANIZATION FOR THE REFORM
OF MARIJUANA LAWS (NORML)

NORML is the principal national organization dedicated to ending "marijuana prohibition" by advocating the decriminalization and legalization of marijuana. NORML supports the removal of all penalties for the private possession of marijuana by adults, cultivation for personal use, and the casual nonprofit transfers of small amounts. NORML also supports the development of a legally controlled market for marijuana.

http://www.norml.org

THE DRUG REFORM COORDINATION NETWORK

The Drug Reform Coordination Network is an organization of concerned citizens working for drug policy reform from a variety of perspectives, including harm reduction, reform of sentencing and forfeiture laws, and the medicalization of some drugs. The organization is also dedicated to the creation, expansion, and continued existence of syringe exchange programs as a proven method of stopping the transmission of blood-borne pathogens in the injecting, drug-using community.

http://www.drcnet.org

D.E.A. DRUG ENFORCEMENT ADMINISTRATION—
U.S. DEPARTMENT OF JUSTICE

The mission of the Drug Enforcement Administration (DEA) is to enforce the controlled substances laws and regulations of the United States and bring to the criminal and civil justice system of the United States, or any other competent jurisdiction, those organizations and principal members of organizations involved in the growing, manufacture, or distribution of controlled substances appearing in or destined for illicit traffic in the United States; and to recommend and support nonenforcement programs aimed at reducing the availability of illicit controlled substances on the domestic and international markets.

http://www.usdoj.gov/dea

HUMAN RIGHTS 95

Human Rights 95 is a photo project/exhibit dedicated to the prisoners of the drug war, their families, and to those who are working to regain their freedom and restore respect for all human rights. HR95 is composed of case studies—including photos and stories—provided by nonviolent prisoners of the drug war who feel their penalties are unjust.

http://www.hr95.org

Are Prisons the Best Way to Deal with Criminals?

In 1980 there were about 500,000 inmates in jails and prisons in the United States. Since then, this number has increased by more than 400 percent, and there are more than 2 million adults in prison or jail today (555 per 100,000 citizens). No other industrialized nation even comes close to this ratio. The imprisonment rate in the United States is five times that of Canada and Australia and seven times that of most European democracies.

Much of the recent increase in these rates results from an increase in the probability of being prosecuted, convicted, and sent to prison following an arrest. In the past ten years, prisoners served longer sentences, too. During that period, the median time for those serving a prison term for a violent index crime increased from 20 months to 25 months.

Many people believe that crime prevention is achieved through incapacitation and imprisonment. The concept of incapacitation is simple—for as long as offenders are in prison, crime is reduced because the offenders are prevented from committing crimes in the community. During the mid-1970s, interest in incapacitation as a crime prevention strategy grew, in part due to concerns about whether rehabilitation methods worked, rising crime rates, and public fear of crime.

Those who believe our imprisonment strategy is working point to the fact that the overall rate of serious crime in the United States fell to a 30-year low in 1999. The murder rate—the number of murders per 100,000 population—dropped to the rates of the late 1960s, even falling below the average murder rate for the entire twentieth century. Not only the murder rate, but also the actual number of murders reported in 1999 was the lowest in more than two decades. Other violent crimes and burglary also showed a decline in 1999. In addition, the National Crime Victimization

Survey, conducted annually by the Justice Department since 1973, found the lowest crime rates since the survey began.

What happened in 1999 continued a trend that started in the 1980s, a trend that accelerated in the 1990s: There is less crime in the United States, as measured by both the crime rate and the actual number of crimes.

Steve H. Hanke and Howard Baetjer, in "Doing Time Chills Crime," argue that even at $30,000 a year, keeping the "average" criminal in prison is worthwhile, since an increase in the prison population reduces all major categories of violent and nonviolent crime. They point to studies that show that on average, about 15 crimes per year are eliminated for each additional prisoner locked up. For serious crimes, therefore, imprisonment pays for itself. These numbers only take crime prevention into account, and underestimate any other benefits of prison to society, such as deterrence of other criminals or a reduction in the suffering of victims.

Hanke and Baetjer also believe the probability of punishment should be increased, a goal that can be accomplished by more and better policing and by higher conviction rates. The punishments for convicted criminals should be increased by lengthening and/or mandating tough sentences and by requiring restitution for victims.

The success of incapacitation in reducing crime in the community remains a controversial subject. Questions arise over how broadly the incapacitation strategy should be used and whether it is a cost-efficient and effective crime prevention strategy. Some think prison space should be reserved for only a small, carefully selected group of dangerous repeat offenders. Most hardened criminals are still paroled well before they have served out their latest sentence behind bars. On any given day in America, there are three convicted adult criminals out on probation or parole for every one in prison—and many of these are indistinguishable (in terms of their violent and repeat criminal histories) from those who remain in prison.

Craig Haney and Philip Zimbardo, in "The Past and Future of U.S. Prison Policy," express alarm at the United States finding itself in the midst of the worst corrections crisis in its history. They lament the fact that "there appear to be no limits on the amount of prison pain the public is willing to inflict in the name of crime control." It is time to fight against this trend and stop using prisons exclusively as agencies of social control that punish without attempting to rehabilitate. Rehabilitation strategies focus on changing individual offenders so they will not continue their criminal activities. Haney and Zimbardo ask us not to give up on what they believe is a more moral way to deal with inmates.

Yes

Doing Time Chills Crime

Steve H.
Hanke and
Howard Baetjer

The FBI recently released data showing that serious crimes decreased in 1996, continuing a pattern that began in 1992. This might satisfy the statisticians who detect an improving trend, but it won't calm the fears of most Americans. Indeed, polls show that the average citizen worries a lot about crime.

Sensing the public's angst, politicians of all stripes have proposed solutions. Their crime-fighting proposals have come in two forms. One is served up by incentivists and the other by structuralists. The incentivists claim that more severe punishments reduce crime rates.

The structuralists object to these solutions. They argue that getting tough on crime doesn't work. For the structuralists, the solution to crime lies in criminal rehabilitation and also in the amelioration of the root cause of crime: the breakdown in moral standards and civility in America.

Who is right? The evidence, which is summarized by James Q. Wilson and Richard Herrnstein in *Crime and Human Nature*, overwhelmingly favors the incentivists. Contrary to assertions made by the structuralists, getting tough on crime works and it works rapidly, according to data presented in the book.

The data also suggest that structuralists err in claiming that criminal rehabilitation works. In actuality, it has a poor track record. The one strong leg structuralists have to stand on is based on their desire to reset the nation's moral compass. This is important. But even if we wear the rosiest of glasses, we cannot be too sanguine about the possibility of changing America's moral standards, at least in the short run.

To reduce crime now, we must change the incentives faced by potential

From *The World & I* (March 1997). Copyright © 1997. Reprinted with the permission of *The World & I*, a publication of The Washington Times Corporation.

criminals. As Gary Becker, the University of Chicago's Nobel-laureate economist, has shown, crimes are not irrational acts. Instead, they are voluntarily committed by people who compare the expected benefits of crime with the expected costs. As Meyer Lansky, the infamous Mafia boss, claimed, "I am a businessman." He calculated the benefits and costs of his actions like everyone else.

To the extent that expected benefits outweigh expected costs, more crime will be committed. This commonsense view is consistent with public opinion, the views of criminals themselves, and a large body of statistical research.

Crime and Expected Punishment

So, one way to reduce crime is to lower its expected payoff, where the payoff is the difference between benefits and costs of criminal activity. Public policy can do nothing about the expected benefits of a crime, but it can do a lot about the expected costs.

Those costs can be measured by determining the expected punishment associated with various criminal acts. That expected punishment is calculated by first multiplying four probabilities: that of being arrested for a crime after it is committed, that of being prosecuted if arrested, that of being convicted if prosecuted, and that of receiving punishment if convicted. The product of that arithmetic is the probability of being punished.

To complete the calculation of expected punishment, we must next multiply the probability of being punished times the penalty for an offense, which is measured by the length of prison sentences and/or the size of restitution payments.

Consider burglary, for example. Of the burglaries committed, less than 7 percent result in an arrest. Of those arrested, 90 percent are prosecuted. Of those prosecuted, 53 percent are convicted. Of those convicted, 42 percent are sent to prison. If we multiply those probabilities together, we find that a burglar has only a 1.4 percent probability of doing prison time.

Because the average prison time for burglars is 15 months, the technical expected punishment is an average of only 6 days in prison (1.4 percent times 15 months). Consequently, a burglary pays if the prospective thief values the stolen goods more than 6 days of freedom.

The National Center for Policy Analysis in Dallas keeps tabs on trends in expected prison time (the expected punishment) for serious crimes.... Several points are worth highlighting:

- Expected punishments, measured by expected prison time, are shockingly light. It's no wonder, according to the figures, that we have so much crime in America.
- The expected punishments were dramatically reduced in the 1960s and '70s. Those were the decades when prisoners' rights were aggressively

pursued. They were also the decades in which America witnessed an explosion in crime rates and the apparent validation of the incentivists' ideas about crime.

- The figures also appear to explain why crime has stayed unacceptably high in the 1980s and '90s. The expected punishments have increased little from their low points in the '70s. Consequently, the expected punishments for all serious crimes, except murder, remain far short of their 1960 levels, at only 3 months for forcible rape, 1 month for robbery, 11 days for aggravated assault, and 6 days for burglary.

With the costs of crime so low, it makes sense, on the basis of a rational benefit/cost analysis, that many people choose to engage in a lot of criminal activity.

Many observers, therefore, say that the solution to America's crime problems is obvious: increase the expected costs of engaging in criminal activity. This can be accomplished by raising the likelihood of punishment and the severity of penalties for criminal offenses.

Incarceration Rates and Crime Rates

This conclusion, of course, is not universally accepted. Indeed, many people embrace the structuralist notion that harsh penalties don't reduce crime rates.

To support their beliefs, they point out that between 1973 and 1994 incarceration rates nearly tripled, while the number of reported violent crimes per capita approximately doubled and the rate of reported property crimes rose by about 30 percent. Consequently, they conclude that incarceration isn't an effective method of fighting crime.

But incentivists find this argument unconvincing. It is based, they say, on what the famous statistician George Yule called a "nonsense correlation."

Harvard University economist Steven Levitt demonstrated in the May 1996 issue of the *Quarterly Journal of Economics* that the increased incarceration rates between 1973 and 1994 suppressed what would have been an even greater explosion in crime, absent increased rates of incarceration. Levitt's careful empirical analysis established a strong relationship between increased incarceration rates and reductions in crime.

His work shows that if we had imprisoned no additional criminals since 1973, America's violent crime rate would be approximately 70 percent higher today and property crime would be almost 50 percent more frequent. Levitt's research suggests that crime in America has risen since 1973 and stays high because we put too few criminals behind bars.

... [A]n increase in the prison population reduces all major categories of violent and nonviolent crime. Using the Harvard economist's data, we can tell just how well prisons work. For each 1,000-inmate increase in the prison population, Levitt's research indicates, the following annual reductions in crime will follow: murders, 4; rapes, 53; assaults, 1,200; robberies, 1,100;

burglaries, 2,600; larcenies, 9,200; and auto thefts, 700. On average, about 15 crimes per year are eliminated for each additional prisoner locked up, Levitt says.

Anecdotes from the States

Evidence from California and Texas, our two most populous states, appears to confirm Levitt's analysis. According to Morgan Reynolds of Texas A&M University, California nearly tripled its imprisonment rate in the 1980s, from 98 to 283 prisoners per 100,000 population. The result was a 26 percent reduction in the rate of violent crime and burglary during the decade, from 3,210 to 2,377 per 100,000 population.

Meanwhile, in Texas, the prisoners per 100,000 population increased only modestly, from 210 to 257. Although this 22 percent increase in the incarceration rate slowed the rate of increase in criminal activity, it was too small to reverse the trend. Indeed, the rate of violent crime and burglary increased by 17 percent during the 1980s in Texas, from 2,403 to 2,810 per 100,000 population.

In the 1990s, the policies of California and Texas flip-flopped, with California becoming more lax and Texas becoming much tougher on crime. Between 1990 and 1994, California increased its imprisonment rate only 23 percent, from 311 to 382 prisoners per 100,000 population. Its crime rate increased also, about 0.5 percent, from 2,391 to 2,405 per 100,000 population.

At the same time, Texas decided to get tough on crime, increasing its imprisonment rate by 88 percent, from 290 to 545 per 100,000, the highest in the nation. In consequence, the crime rates in Texas fell by 21 percent, from 2,613 to 2,059 per 100,000 population.

Incarceration seems to work in Europe, too. For example, British Home Secretary Michael Howard reports that a reduction in crime rates of 8.5 percent over the last three years has been associated with a 25 percent increase in Britain's prison population over the last three and a half years.

Research by Britain's Home Office also squares with Levitt's findings for America: Keeping a British burglar in prison for a year eliminates between 3 and 13 offenses.

Do Prisons Pay?

Incarceration, therefore, appears to work. But does it pay? Levitt's figures suggest that prisons are among the best public investments America can make. He first estimates the economic benefit to society of keeping bad guys behind bars—that is, the annual amount of damage the average criminal would do if on the loose: $53,900.

From this benefit, Levitt subtracts the annual cost to taxpayers of incarceration, about $30,000 per prisoner. This yields an average net benefit of $23,900 per year for each criminal behind bars.

The economist's study thus shows incarceration to be a bargain. Indeed, it could easily be made more so. If inmates were required to work while in prison, they could pay for at least part of their keep. By reducing the taxpayer-financed costs of prison, prison-work mandates would make incarceration an even more attractive bargain.

Many analysts believe that if Americans want to be serious about immediately reducing crime, the solutions are at hand. They say that:

- The probability of punishments should be increased, a goal that can be accomplished by more and better policing and by higher conviction rates.

- The punishments for convicted criminals should be increased by lengthening and/or mandating tough sentences and by requiring restitution for victims. Incidentally, according to the incentivists, tougher, mandated sentences should be imposed on criminals who use guns. This targeted approach to gun control, crime experts say, would reduce use of guns by thugs, without increasing the costs of owning and using guns for legitimate purposes.

- Scarce prison space should be allocated primarily to the most dangerous criminals: those with victims. Lengthened and/or mandated sentences, therefore, should target those who commit the most serious crimes and repeat offenders. It makes little sense to use up prison space for a penny-ante criminal who has committed a burglary for the first time if that precludes locking up a serial rapist. Also, serious criminals and repeat offenders should not qualify for early-release programs, if such programs are employed.

- Prisoners should be required to work, so that some of the costs of prisons could be transferred from law-abiding taxpayers to criminals.

To many, this might all sound rather hard-hearted. But a growing number of analysts believe that this package of incentive-based prescriptions would provide immediate relief.

So much for reducing crime rates today. But what about tomorrow? To answer this question, we must address what many researchers believe to be the root cause of crime: the lack of moral standards.

There is little doubt that a wider embrace of a more socially benevolent moral code would do wonders to reduce crime over time. In the 1930s, for example, when a comparatively rectitudinous culture prevailed, few people bothered to lock their doors and theft was generally petty and rare, despite a context of unemployment and poverty that is unimaginable in our wealthy welfare state. "Do unto others as you would have them do unto you" was the order of the day. People took responsibility and expected to be held accountable for their actions.

If we are to have a successful civil society in the long run, we will have to rebuild moral standards so that the vast majority of people honor contracts, respect the rights and property of others, and generally keep their word.

A blueprint to guide this rebuilding effort is, of course, elusive. But it wouldn't hurt if the chattering classes—starting with politicians and extending to journalists, academics, and entertainment figures—upgraded their own moral standards and led by example.

The Past and Future of U.S. Prison Policy

Craig Haney and
Philip Zimbardo

...

The story of how the nature and purpose of imprisonment have been transformed over the past 25 years is very different from the one that we once hoped and expected we would be able to tell. At the time we conducted the SPE—in 1971—there was widespread concern about the fairness and the efficacy of the criminal justice system. Scholars, politicians, and members of the public wondered aloud whether prisons were too harsh, whether they adequately rehabilitated prisoners, and whether there were alternatives to incarceration that would better serve correctional needs and interests. Many states were already alarmed about increased levels of overcrowding. Indeed, in those days, prisons that operated at close to 90 percent of capacity were thought to be dangerously overcrowded. It was widely understood by legislators and penologists alike that under such conditions, programming resources were stretched too thin, and prison administrators were left with increasingly fewer degrees of freedom with which to respond to interpersonal conflicts and a range of other inmate problems.

Despite these concerns about overcrowding, there was a functional moratorium on prison construction in place in most parts of the country. Whatever else it represented, the moratorium reflected a genuine skepticism at some of the very highest levels of government about the viability of prison as a solution to the crime problem. Indeed, the report of the National Advisory Commission on Criminal Justice Standards and Goals (1973) ... concluded that prisons, juvenile reformatories, and jails had achieved what it

From *American Psychologist* 53 (July 1998). Copyright © 1998 by the American Psychological Association, Inc. Reprinted with the permission of the authors and the American Psychological Association.

characterized as a "shocking record of failure," suggested that these institutions may have been responsible for creating more crime than they prevented, and recommended that the moratorium on prison construction last at least another 10 years.

To be sure, there was a fiscal undercurrent to otherwise humanitarian attempts to avoid the overuse of imprisonment. Prisons are expensive, and without clear evidence that they worked very well, it was difficult to justify building and running more of them. But there was also a fair amount of genuine concern among the general public about what was being done to prisoners behind prison walls and what the long-term effects would be.

...

The late 1960s saw the beginning of a prisoners' rights movement that eventually raised the political consciousness of large numbers of prisoners, some of whom became effective spokespersons for their cause. Widely publicized, tragic events in several prisons in different parts of the country vividly illustrated how prisoners could be badly mistreated by prison authorities and underscored the potentially serious drawbacks of relying on prisons as the centerpiece in a national strategy of crime control.

...

Subsequent revelations about the use of excessive force and an official cover-up contributed to public skepticism about prisons and doubts about the wisdom and integrity of some of their administrators.

...

And then, almost without warning, all of this critical reappraisal and constructive optimism about humane standards and alternatives to incarceration was replaced with something else. The counterrevolution in crime and punishment began slowly and imperceptibly at first and then pushed forward with a consistency of direction and effect that could not be overlooked. It moved so forcefully and seemingly inexorably during the 1980s that it resembled nothing so much as a runaway punishment train, driven by political steam and fueled by media-induced fears of crime.

...

Our nation finds itself in the midst of arguably the worst corrections crisis in U.S. history, with every indication that it will get worse before it can possibly get better. For the first time in the 200-year history of imprisonment in the United States, there appear to be no limits on the amount of prison pain the public is willing to inflict in the name of crime control. Retired judge Lois Forer, in her denunciation of some of these recent trends, warned of the dire consequences of what she called the "rage to punish." But this rage has been indulged so completely that it threatens to override any of the competing concerns for humane justice that once served to make this system more compassionate and fair. The United States has entered what another commentator called the "mean season" of corrections, one in which penal philosophy amounts to little more than devising "creative strategies to make offenders suffer."

...

The Death of Rehabilitation

A dramatic shift in correctional philosophy was pivotal to the series of changes that followed. Almost overnight, the concept that had served as the intellectual cornerstone of corrections policy for nearly a century—rehabilitation—publicly and politically discredited. The country moved abruptly in the mid-1970s from a society that justified putting people in prison on the basis of the belief that their incarceration would somehow facilitate their productive reentry into the free world to one that used imprisonment merely to disable criminal offenders ("incapacitation") or to keep them far away from the rest of society ("containment"). At a more philosophical level, imprisonment was now said to further something called "just desserts"—locking people up for no other reason than they deserved it and for no other purpose than to punish them. In fact, prison punishment soon came to be thought of as its own reward, serving only the goal of inflicting pain.

Determinate Sentencing and the Politicizing of Prison Pain

Almost simultaneously—and, in essence, as a consequence of the abandonment of rehabilitation—many states moved from indeterminate to determinate models of prison sentencing. Because indeterminate sentencing had been devised as a mechanism to allow for the release of prisoners who were rehabilitated early—and the retention of those whose in-prison change took longer—it simply did not fit with the new goals of incarceration. This shift to determinate sentencing did have the intended consequence of removing discretion from the hands of prison administrators and even judges who, studies showed, from time to time abused it. However, it also had the likely unintended consequence of bringing prison sentencing into an openly political arena. Once largely the province of presumably expert judicial decision makers, prison administrators, or parole authorities who operated largely out of the public view, prison sentencing had remained relatively free from at least the most obvious and explicit forms of political influence. They no longer were. Moreover, determinate sentencing and the use of rigid sentencing guidelines or "grids" undermined the role of situation and context in the allocation of punishment.

The Imprisoning of America

The moratorium on new prison construction that was in place at the time of the SPE was ended by the confluence of several separate, powerful forces. For one, legislators continued to vie for the mantle of "toughest on crime" by regularly increasing the lengths of prison sentences. Of course, this meant that prisoners were incarcerated for progressively longer periods of time. In addition, the sentencing discretion of judges was almost completely subjugated to the various aforementioned legislative grids, formulas, and guidelines. Moreover, the advent of determinate sentencing meant that prison administrators had no outlets at the other end of this flow of prisoners to relieve population pressures (which, under indeterminate sentencing, had been discretionary). Finally, federal district court judges began to enter judicial orders that prohibited states from, among other things, cramming two and three or more prisoners into one-person (typically six feet by nine feet) cells. Eventually even long-time opponents of new prisons agreed that prisoners could no longer be housed in these shockingly inadequate spaces and reluctantly faced the inevitable: Prison construction began on an unprecedented scale across the country.

Although this rapid prison construction briefly eased the overcrowding problem, prisoner populations continued to grow at unprecedented rates (see Figure 1). It soon became clear that even dramatic increases in the number of new prisons could not keep pace. In fact, almost continuously over the past 25 years, penologists have described U.S. prisons as "in crisis" and have characterized each new level of overcrowding as "unprecedented." As the decade of the 1980s came to a close, the United States was imprisoning more people for longer periods of time than ever before in our history, far surpassing other industrialized democracies in the use of incarceration as a crime control measure. As of June 1997, the most recent date for which figures are available, the total number of persons incarcerated in the United States exceeded 1.7 million (Bureau of Justice Statistics, 1998), which continues the upward trend of the previous 11 years, from 1985 to 1996, when the number rose from 744,208 to 1,630,940. Indeed, 10 years ago, long before today's record rates were attained, one scholar concluded, "It is easily demonstrable that America's use of prison is excessive to the point of barbarity, with a prison rate several times higher than that of other similarly developed Western countries."

…

The push to higher rates and lengths of incarceration has only intensified since then. Most state and federal prisons now operate well above their rated capacities, with many overcrowded to nearly twice their design limits. At the start of the 1990s, the United States incarcerated more persons per capita than any other modern nation in the world. The international disparities are most striking when the U.S. incarceration rate is contrasted to those of other nations with which the United States is often compared, such as Japan, The Netherlands, Australia, and the United Kingdom; throughout most of the present decade, the U.S. rates have consistently been between four and eight times as high as those of these other nations.

Figure 1   Number of Prisoners in the United States, 1970–1995

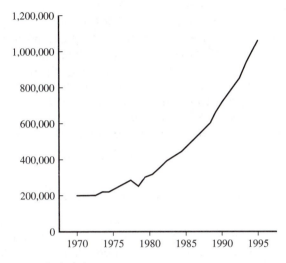

Note: Jail inmates are not included.

The increase in U.S. prison populations during these years was not produced by a disproportionate increase in the incarceration of violent offenders. In 1995, only one-quarter of persons sentenced to state prisons were convicted of a violent offense, whereas three quarters were sent for property or drug offenses or other nonviolent crimes such as receiving stolen property or immigration violations (Bureau of Justice Statistics, 1996). Nor was the increased use of imprisonment related to increased levels of crime. In fact, according to the National Crime Victimization Survey, conducted by the Bureau of the Census, a survey of 94,000 U.S. residents found that many fewer of them were the victims of crime during the calendar year 1995–1996, the year our incarceration rate reached an all-time high (Bureau of Justice Statistics, 1997b).

The Racialization of Prison Pain

The aggregate statistics describing the extraordinary punitiveness of the U.S. criminal justice system mask an important fact: The pains of imprisonment have been inflicted disproportionately on minorities, especially black men. Indeed, for many years, the rate of incarceration of white men in the United States compared favorably with those in most Western European nations, including countries regarded as the most progressive and least punitive. Although in recent years the rate of incarceration for whites in the United States has also increased and no longer compares favorably with other Western European nations, it still does not begin to approximate the rate for African Americans. Thus, although they represent less than 6 percent of the general U.S. population, African-American men constitute 48 percent of those confined to state prisons. Statistics collected at the beginning of this decade indicated that blacks were more than six times more likely to be imprisoned than their white counterparts. By 1995, that disproportion had grown to seven and one-half times (Bureau of Justice Statistics, 1996). In fact, the United States incarcerates African-American men at a rate that is approximately four times the rate of incarceration of black men in South Africa.

...

The Overincarceration of Drug Offenders

The increasingly disproportionate number of African-American men who are being sent to prison seems to be related to the dramatic increase in the number of persons incarcerated for drug-related offenses, combined with the greater tendency to imprison black drug offenders as compared with their white counterparts. Thus, although blacks and whites use drugs at approximately the same rate (Bureau of Justice Statistics, 1991), African Americans were arrested for drug offenses during the so-called war on drugs at a much higher rate than were whites. The most recent data show that between 1985 and 1995, the number of African Americans incarcerated in state prisons due to drug violations (which were their only or their most serious offense) rose 707 percent.... In contrast, the number of whites incarcerated in state prisons for drug offenses (as their only or most serious offense) underwent a 306 percent change. In 1986, for example, only 7 percent of black prison inmates in the United States had been convicted of drug crimes, compared with 8 percent of whites. By 1991, however, the black percentage had more than tripled to 25 percent, whereas the percentage of white inmates incarcerated for drug crimes had increased by only half to 12 percent. In the federal prison system, the numbers of African Americans incarcerated for drug violations are shockingly high: Fully 64 percent of male and 71 percent of female black prisoners incarcerated in federal institutions in 1995 had been sent there for drug offenses (Bureau of Justice Statistics, 1996).

...

As we noted, the types and proportions of offenses for which people were incarcerated in the United States were highly consistent for the 75 years prior to 1984. For most of the twentieth century, the U.S. prison population consisted of around 60–70 percent offenders against property, 13–24 percent offenders against persons (now called violent crime), around 20 percent public order–morals violations (which included drug offenses), and 10 percent other types of offenders.

However, these distributions have changed dramatically during the past

10 to 15 years. The federal government is now willing to incarcerate people for a wider range of criminal violations, and both state and federal prisoners remain incarcerated for longer periods of time. The number of violent offenders who are incarcerated has risen but not as steeply as the number of drug offenders who are now sent to prison.

...

We note in passing that these three interrelated trends—the extraordinary increase in the numbers of persons in prison, the disproportionate incarceration of minorities, and the high percentage of persons incarcerated for drug offenses—reflect a consistent disregard of context and situation in the criminal justice policies of the past 25 years. The unprecedented use of imprisonment per se manifests a policy choice to incarcerate individual lawbreakers instead of targeting the criminogenic social conditions and risk factors that have contributed to their criminality. Sentencing models that ignore situation and context inevitably lead to higher rates of incarceration among groups of citizens who confront race-based poverty and deprivation and other social ills that are related to discrimination. The failure to address the differential opportunity structure that leads young minority group members into certain kinds of drug-related activities and the conscious decision to target those activities for criminal prosecution and incarceration, rather than to attempt to improve the life chances of the urban black underclass, reflect dispositional—and discriminatory—views of crime control.

Moreover, excessive and disproportionate use of imprisonment ignores the secondary effects that harsh criminal justice policies eventually will have on the social contexts and communities from which minority citizens come. Remarkably, as the present decade began, there were more young black men (between the ages of 20 and 29) under the control of the nation's criminal justice system (including probation and parole supervision) than the total number in college. Thus, one scholar has predicted that "imprisonment will become the most significant factor contributing to the dissolution and breakdown of African-American families during the decade of the 1990s," and another has concluded that "crime control policies are a major contributor to the disruption of the family, the prevalence of single parent families, and children raised without a father in the ghetto, and the 'inability of people to get the jobs still available.'"

The Rise of the "Supermax" Prison

In addition to becoming dangerously overcrowded and populated by a disproportionate number of minority citizens and drug offenders over the past 25 years, many U.S. prisons also now lack meaningful work, training, education, treatment, and counseling programs for the prisoners who are confined in them. Plagued by increasingly intolerable living conditions where prisoners serve long sentences that they now have no hope of having reduced through "good time" credits, due to laws imposed by state legislatures, many prison officials have turned to punitive policies of within-prison segregation in the hope of maintaining institutional control.

...

Here, too, the importance of context and situation has been ignored. Widespread prison management problems and gang-related infractions are best understood in systematic terms, as at least in large part the products of worsening overall institutional conditions. Viewing them instead as caused exclusively by "problem prisoners" who require nothing more than isolated and segregated confinement ignores the role of compelling situational forces that help to account for their behavior. It also overlooks the capacity of deteriorated prison conditions to continue to generate new replacements who will assume the roles of those prisoners who have been taken to segregation. Finally, the continued use of high levels of punitive isolation, despite evidence of significant psychological trauma and psychiatric risk, reflects a legal failure to fully appreciate the costs of these potentially harmful social contexts—both in terms of immediate pain and emotional damage as well as their long-term effects on post-segregation and even post-release behavior.

...

Where has this series of transformations left the U.S. criminal justice system? With startling speed, national prison policy has become remarkably punitive, and correspondingly, conditions of confinement have dramatically deteriorated in many parts of the country. These transformations have been costly in economic, social, and human terms. At the beginning of the present decade, a stark fact about governmental priorities was reported: "For the first time in history, state and municipal governments are spending more money on criminal justice than education." In California, the corrections budget alone has now surpassed the state's fiscal outlays for higher education. Despite this historic shift in expenditures and the unprecedented prison construction that took place during the past 25 years, many commentators still lament what has been referred to as the "national scandal of living conditions in American prisons." As we have noted and one reviewer recently observed, "For over a decade, virtually every contemporary commentary on corrections in the United States has reminded us that the system [is] in crisis."

...

There has never been a more critical time at which to begin the intellectual struggle with those who would demean human nature by using prisons exclusively as agencies of social control that punish without attempting to rehabilitate, that isolate and oppress instead of educating and elevating, and that tear down minority communities rather than protecting and strengthening them.

Key Websites

BUREAU OF JUSTICE STATISTICS—SOURCEBOOK OF CRIMINAL JUSTICE STATISTICS ONLINE

The *Sourcebook of Criminal Justice Statistics* brings together data about all aspects of criminal justice in the United States, presented in over 600 tables from more than 100 sources. Most recently, this site presented the 27th edition of *Sourcebook*, published in the summer of 2000. Although the publication of *Sourcebook* is an annual event, its compilation is an ongoing process. As such, updates of tables and new data sources are continually posted.
http://www.albany.edu/sourcebook

BUREAU OF JUSTICE STATISTICS—NATIONAL PRISONER STATISTICS

This site contains annual and semiannual national and state-level data on the numbers of prisoners in state and federal prison facilities. Since 1926, the federal government has published data annually on the prisoner count in each state, the District of Columbia, and the federal prison system.
http://www.ojp.usdoj.gov/bjs/pud/pdf/mpc.pdf

U.S. DEPARTMENT OF JUSTICE, NATIONAL INSTITUTE OF CORRECTIONS—NIC INFORMATION CENTER

This site provides access to downloadable corrections research publications; a database of materials produced by NIC or with NIC support; information on NIC research assistance; a public listserv for discussion of corrections issues; a description of the only federal library collection focused on corrections issues; and links to selected corrections-related websites.
http://www.nicic.org

FEDERAL BUREAU OF PRISONS—NATIONAL INSTITUTE OF CORRECTIONS

This site contains information on federal prisons, inmates, and jobs available at the Federal Bureau of Prisons. The site also has links to topic papers and other sites.
http://www.bop.gov

OTHER SIDE OF THE WALL

This extensive site is devoted to prisoner rights and prison issues. It contains numerous links to articles, writing by inmates, poems, books, and songs.
http://www.wco.com/~aerick/prison.html

PRIVATE PRISONS—THE PRISON PRIVATIZATION RESEARCH SITE

This site contains tables, charts, figures, and reports on private prisons. Although it presents arguments both for and against private prisons, it was designed by an advocate of private prisons. This is an excellent starting point for research on this topic.
http://www.ucc.uconn.edu/~logan

THE CORRECTIONS CONNECTION NETWORK

This site bills itself as "The Official Site of the Correction Industry." It is devoted entirely to correctional news and products and advances in security. The site contains information on books, videos, and technology related to corrections. It also has numerous links to a wide variety of corrections topics.
http://www.corrections.com

FEDERAL BUREAU OF PRISONS—OFFICE OF RESEARCH AND EVALUATION

The mission of the Office of Research and Evaluation (ORE) is to provide information relevant to current and future questions in the field of corrections by conducting social science research. ORE's primary functions include conducting policy analyses, performing evaluative and basic research studies, developing and maintaining information systems, producing technical and statistical reports, responding to information requests, providing technical assistance, and reviewing and processing research proposals.
http://www.bop.gov

Are Some People Born Criminals?

At one time, a child's behavior was thought to be mainly, if not entirely, the result of how his or her parents behaved. Nice parents produced nice children; bad parents produced bad children. The pioneering study of delinquents written by Sheldon and Eleanor Glueck in the 1950s made it clear that those poor parents created juvenile offenders.

Now some people are starting to suggest that biology and genes play an important role in the origins of criminality. Byron M. Roth, in "Crime and Child-Rearing," argues that research provides considerable support for the idea that criminals are born rather than made; genes appear to count far more than upbringing. He notes that criminal behavior is associated with personality traits that have been shown to have a high degree of heritability. These include intelligence, impulse control, and aggressiveness. They can be identified in relatively young children and are resilient to environmental manipulation. When low levels of intelligence and impulse control are combined with aggressiveness there is a good chance of criminal behavior. He believes that very few children are destined to be criminals because of inherited traits, but many with traits that put them at risk will gravitate toward criminality.

A belief in the power of genes diminishes the importance of such personal qualities as free will and a sense of responsibility for personal choices—if it's in your genes, you're not accountable. It allows the criminal, for example, to treat himself as a helpless victim of his biology rather than as an individual with control of his own behavior.

Discussion about the role of genes in behavior is not new. The term eugenics was coined in 1883 by Sir Francis Galton, Charles Darwin's cousin, to refer to those born "good in stock, hereditarily endowed with noble qualities." The goal was the improvement of the human race through better breeding. To both men, better breeding implied improving the quality of the human species using the findings of modern science, particularly the science of heredity.

The eugenics movement was fueled at least in part by a desire to get rid of habitual criminals, and many attempts have been made over the years to identify genetic roots for aggression, violence, and criminality. Eugenicists argued that if unemployment and crime resulted from the behavior of genetically inadequate persons, then clearly the most rational solution was to prevent those types from being born in the first place. It was inefficient, they contended, to allow the biologically degenerate and unfit to reproduce, merely to fill the insane asylums, hospitals, and prisons with defective people that the state must support the rest of their lives.

When most people think about heredity, they think in terms of one gene, one trait. But for most complex human behaviors, this is far from true. A more accurate view involves many different genes, some of which control other genes, and many of which are controlled by signals from the environment. Herbert Wray, in "Politics of Biology: How the Nature vs. Nurture Debate Shapes Public Policy—and Our View of Ourselves," points out that crime and alcohol abuse are so entangled that it's often difficult to know whether genetic markers are associated with drinking, criminality, or something else entirely, like a personality trait. Getting from those unknown genes to an actual act of vandalism or assault—or a life of barbaric violence—requires an enormous leap of faith. Yet it's a leap that many are willing to make.

Wray notes that the relative contributions of genes and the environment are so thoroughly dynamic and enduring that to ask what's more important, nature or nurture, is like asking what's more important to a rectangle, its length or its width. The emerging view of nature–nurture is that many complicated behaviors probably have some measure of genetic predisposition for schizophrenia, for instance, or for aggression. But then the nurture factor takes over and, just as bad experiences can influence certain genes, rich and challenging experiences have the power to enhance life, again acting through the genes. The way to intervene in human lives and improve them, to ameliorate mental illness, addictions, and criminal behavior, is to enrich impoverished environments, to improve conditions in the family and society.

Yes

Crime and Child-Rearing

Byron M. Roth

Recent research provides considerable support for the idea, long despised, that criminals are born rather than made; genes appear to count far more than upbringing.

Studies of identical twins, involving thousands of cases in Europe, America, and Australia, provide striking support for the hereditarian case. Traits such as intelligence, aggressiveness, impulse control, optimism, and many other things, even political orientation, appear to be strongly affected by a person's genetic makeup.

...

Competent parents can influence their children's development by allowing them to explore their strengths and weaknesses and can, with proper intervention, prevent the foreclosure of future possibilities by immature choices and actions. These efforts by parents can be complemented by schools, which can, to some extent, compensate for less competent parents. But neither parents nor schools seem capable of changing a child's IQ, of turning an optimistic child into a pessimist, or an introverted child into an extrovert.

By the same token, inadequate child-rearing does not appear to block the expression of valuable traits and abilities in children. Even being raised in a seriously abusive home, contrary to common understandings, does not appreciably increase the chances of a child becoming delinquent. In the most comprehensive study to date on delinquency and child abuse, Matthew Zingraff and fellow researchers at North Carolina State University found no significant relationship between the two. Decades of research on illegitimacy and single parenthood have likewise failed to support the popular idea that

From *Society* (November 21, 1996). Copyright © 1996 by Transaction Publishers. Reprinted with the permission of the publishers. All rights reserved.

61

the absence of a father is a significant source of criminality. When important factors—such as the genetic similarities between parent and child—are controlled, single parenthood does not appear to be a major source of delinquency. Temperamental differences among children are detectable at an early age and are quite stable.

...

Criminal behavior is associated with personality traits that have been shown to have a high degree of heritability. Intelligence, impulse control, and aggressivity are such traits; they can be identified in relatively young children and are resilient to environmental manipulation. When they appear in combination they are highly correlated with criminality.

This latter assertion is based in part on recent highly acclaimed research by University of Wisconsin psychologist Terrie Moffitt and her coworkers. This ongoing research involves a comprehensive longitudinal study of a New Zealand birth cohort. Children were tested, and parents and children interviewed, at regular intervals from birth until age 18. Moffitt and her fellow researchers found that children with chronic histories of delinquency exhibit characteristic trait patterns, of which the most important appear to be low intelligence, especially in verbal abilities, deficient impulse control, and irritable or aggressive temperament. The results of this ongoing study are similar to others in finding that while large numbers of adolescents exhibit delinquent behavior, relatively few graduate to become career criminals. Moffitt differentiates between childhood-onset delinquents, who have histories of problem behavior going back to early childhood, and adolescent-onset delinquents, who have no such troubled childhoods.

Adolescent-onset delinquency is quite common; approximately 25 percent of the New Zealand cohort engaged in a large number of delinquent acts. Moffitt suggests that such behavior is an extreme form of the more or less normal response of young males to the social restrictions on their emerging maturity. She thinks these people have a fairly good prognosis since they seem relatively well-adjusted despite their delinquency. The main danger to their future, in Moffitt's view, is that they may be undermined by drug addiction, interrupted education, lengthy incarceration, or debilitating injuries.

Childhood-onset delinquency is far less common, representing 7 percent of the cohort, but the prognosis for these adolescents appears less sanguine. While both groups engaged in considerable criminal behavior, the child-onset offenders were three times as likely to have been convicted of a violent crime, and they committed those crimes at a much younger age than the adolescent-onset offenders.

Perhaps the most serious impediment confronting the child-onset offenders is their lack of intellectual resources. The average IQ of this group was 17 points below the average of the entire cohort. The average IQ of the adolescent-onset delinquents, in contrast, was only one point below the average. These findings are consistent with those of Richard Herrnstein and

Charles Murray, who reported in *The Bell Curve* that among white males, those with IQs in the bottom 5 percent were 14 times more likely to have been incarcerated than were those in the top 25 percent. They are also consistent with long-standing data indicating that delinquents on average score eight to ten points lower in IQ than nondelinquents. It is important to report that about half of those with histories of behavioral problems as children did not graduate to serious delinquency in adolescence.

The personality traits of the childhood-onset delinquents are similar to those characterized as psychopathic, with the important difference that low IQ is not generally associated with psychopathy. Bruce Pennington and Loisa Bennetto of the University of Denver argue that psychopathic traits are often present in people who have sustained frontal lobe damage. Such damage tends to interfere with foresight, impulse control, and emotional responsiveness. Perhaps many of those diagnosed as psychopaths are suffering from undetected neural deficits.

Psychopaths are particularly egregious in their lack of empathy and conscience. The main difference between the noncriminal psychopath and the sociopathic career criminal may reside in their general intelligence. High IQ people very rarely become career criminals, even if their life experiences and temperamental characteristics put them at risk. On the other hand, many of the most notorious tyrants in history were intellectually brilliant, but psychopathically devoid of empathy. Perhaps a sizable number of career criminals are unintelligent people with psychopathic dispositions. A good many of the world's scoundrels are in all likelihood people with similar dispositions but more intelligence.

...

David Rowe, in his important book *The Limits of Family Influence*, makes the point that many researchers overlook the likely genetic similarities between parent and offspring and mistakenly attribute such similarities to upbringing. Low IQ children, for instance, often grow up in homes without books and other signs of intellectual stimulation. This is offered as evidence that low IQ is the product of an impoverished childhood. But, of course, intelligence is highly heritable, and parents who are less intelligent are also less likely to collect books.

Adopted children tend, in fact, to bear a closer resemblance in IQ to their biological parents than to their adoptive ones, and the resemblance to biological parents becomes stronger as the child grows older. This is most likely because the child is better able to shape his personal environment so as to bring it into line with his interests and abilities. In fact, the most important environmental influences on personality are usually selected by individuals themselves, and these choices are often genetically influenced.

The tendency for individuals to shape their own environments is pervasive. Intelligent children tend to choose intelligent friends, find education rewarding, and read books that are more demanding than those read by their less intelligent counterparts. Similarly, adolescents prone to criminality tend to select friends with similar inclinations. The voluntary clustering of young people into like-minded subgroups is a commonplace of every American high school. Many genetically influenced behaviors may, therefore, be mistakenly attributed to peer influence. For instance, gang membership contributes to criminal conduct, but traits associated with criminality also incline youngsters to join gangs.

Sometimes genetic influences are overlooked because genes produce different effects depending on the presence of other genes. This is clearest in sex-related characteristics. Genes influencing physical size and body shape will operate differently depending on whether they appear in males or females. This appears to be true for behavioral traits as well. According to Rowe, boys who engage in delinquent behavior are more likely to have sisters who are promiscuous at an early age, even after social factors have been controlled. This suggests that delinquency in boys and promiscuity in girls may have common genetic influences.

If genetic factors play an important role in predisposing individuals to criminality, then anything that increases those factors in the gene pool could produce an increase in crime. This is especially so since only a very small proportion of the population engages in violent crime, and any increase in this group will have a marked effect, overall, on crime rates. This is obviously a controversial assertion, but certainly worth considering. Let me emphasize that while crime, overall, is currently on the decline, it is increasing rather dramatically among adolescents, especially younger adolescents. There is, in addition, considerable anecdotal evidence that the crimes committed by adolescents today are startlingly more violent and depraved than those committed in earlier times. Often the perpetrators exhibit a pathological absence of empathy....

Of course, this increased depravity might be the product of incompetent or vicious upbringing, but the evidence on child abuse makes this unlikely. It could, however, be partly the product of changes in mating patterns, especially among the poor, that have taken place in recent decades. The first such change is the increase in illegitimacy. The second is the younger age at which women commence sexual activity.

The rise in illegitimacy, coupled with welfare provisions, has created a pattern in which large numbers of women rear children without the financial support of men. A well-established finding of evolutionary biology is that when paternal care is unnecessary, females tend to be attracted to other things in the males who court them. They tend to, in particular, prefer mates who will provide them with healthy and successful offspring. They look, therefore, for signs of health and physical prowess and, in addition, for features, such as brightly colored plumage, that are attractive to other females. This latter preference is based on the fact that attractive males are more likely to have attractive children, who will, in turn, be more successful in their own sexual endeavors.

The point of the above, as it relates to humans, is that as the financial prospects of potential mates become less important to women, other factors tend to become more important, if only by default. Things such as physical appearance and behavioral flamboyance are likely to take precedence over more mundane considerations. In this regard, today's lower-class adolescent subcultures mirror many premodern societies, which were dominated by aggressive, physically courageous, and often unscrupulous men. The anthropological literature is filled with depictions of such societies, a common feature of which is that dominant men are likely to have more wives and mistresses and therefore more offspring than their weaker peers....

While there is relatively little data on the fathers of today's illegitimate children, flamboyant, risk-taking, aggressive males do seem to be more successful in attracting females. Elijah Anderson, in his study of underclass culture, depicts underclass men as boastful and proud of their willingness to exploit women, who are often young girls. Girls who become sexually active at a young age are especially prone to exploitation by unscrupulous older males. In two-thirds of the births to teenage mothers, the father is over 20, and he is sometimes considerably older than the girl. Some states, such as California and Florida, have become sufficiently alarmed by these statistics that they have begun to reconsider their tolerant policies regarding statutory rape.

If the character traits common among men who exploit women are influenced by inheritance, as they almost certainly are, many of their offspring will share those traits that, when coupled with low IQ, are conducive to criminality. Illegitimate births, in fact, are most common among women with low IQs.... Put bluntly, the mating patterns that have taken hold among poor adolescents seemed designed to increase the proportion of traits conducive to criminality.

The leniency of the juvenile justice system compounds the problem by allowing young criminals to remain in their communities, when in the past they would have been removed to prisons and reform schools. While rarely acknowledged, imprisonment has eugenic effects in preventing reproduction by those deemed socially undesirable, at least during their period of incarceration. Criminals left in neighborhoods are free to court young girls, and it would hardly be surprising to discover that these men are among those who exhibit few qualms about exploiting them.

In contrast to the current patterns, monogamous mating patterns have a democratizing influence on reproduction; in principle, all men, even those with very modest abilities or unexciting traits, have the opportunity to mate if they are able to support families. Flamboyant and aggressive men have few opportunities to reproduce if females are closely monitored by family and neighbors, and are often at a severe reproductive disadvantage if they fail to develop the capacity to support wives and children.

In sum, there have been substantial changes in courtship and mating patterns during recent decades, and these changes have in a variety of ways greatly improved the reproductive prospects of men possessing traits associated with criminality. Perhaps the rising rates of crime and depravity among adolescents are the dysgenic legacy of the new courtship and mating patterns that became the norm some 20 to 30 years ago. If this is even partially correct, then illegitimacy may be tied to crime, but perhaps not so much because children need law-abiding fathers in the home as that they need the genetic traits that law-abiding fathers provide. Of course it would be imprudent to accept this conclusion without serious reservations. On the other hand, it would be equally imprudent to reject it, out of hand, without adequate empirical tests.

. . .

None of the above is meant to deny that seriously deficient mothering caused by drug addiction, alcoholism, or prostitution can have deleterious effects on children. One should not, however, be led astray by the press coverage of truly egregious parental behavior. Very few women are in fact abusive mothers. Poor, uneducated women may be less-adequate parents, but there is no indication that large numbers are lacking in love and concern for their children. It is just as reasonable, in fact more reasonable, to argue that the children of inadequate mothers are more prone to crime because they inherit their mother's or father's inadequacies than that they are driven into crime by those inadequacies.

Caring, consistent, and loving parents are clearly important for children's happiness and well-being. The absence of a father appears to be painful to children in all walks of life. Many children grow up in seriously dysfunctional homes and suffer great unhappiness as a result. But, having said all that, it is nevertheless becoming increasingly clear that few of these family conditions or child-rearing practices have a substantial impact on adult criminality.

. . .

Very few children are destined to be criminals because of inherited traits, but many with traits that put them at risk will gravitate toward criminality if not properly corrected.

Politics of Biology: How the Nature vs. Nurture Debate Shapes Public Policy— and Our View of Ourselves

Herbert Wray

Nearly every week there is a report of a new gene for one trait or another. Novelty seeking, religiosity, shyness, the tendency to divorce, and even happiness (or the lack of it) are among the traits that may result in part from a gene, according to new research.

This cultural shift has political and personal implications. On the personal level, a belief in the power of genes necessarily diminishes the potency of such personal qualities as will, capacity to choose, and sense of responsibility for those choices—if it's in your genes, you're not accountable. It allows the alcoholic, for example, to treat himself as a helpless victim of his biology rather than as a willful agent with control of his own behavior. Genetic determinism can free victims and their families of guilt— or lock them in their suffering.

On the political level, biological determinism now colors all sorts of public-policy debates on issues such as gay rights, health care, juvenile justice, and welfare reform. The effort to dismantle social programs is fueled by the belief that government interventions (the nurturing side in the nature-nurture debate) don't work very well—and the corollary idea that society can't make up for every unfortunate citizen's bad luck....

Even so, genetic determinism can have paradoxical consequences at times, leading to disdain rather than sympathy for the disadvantaged, and marginalization rather than inclusion. Cultural critics are beginning to sort out the unpredictable politics of biology, focusing on four traits: violence, mental illness, alcoholism, and sexual orientation.

From *U.S. News & World Report* (April 21, 1997). Copyright © 1997 by U.S. News and World Report, Inc. Reprinted with the permission of *U.S. News & World Report*. All rights reserved.

The Nature of Violence

To get a sense of just how thorough—and how politicized—the biologizing of culture has been, just look at the issue of urban gang violence as it is framed today. A few years ago, Frederick Goodwin, then director of the government's top mental health agency, was orchestrating the so-called Federal Violence Initiative to identify inner-city kids at biological risk for criminal violence, with the goal of intervening with drug treatments for what are presumed to be nervous-system aberrations. Goodwin got himself fired for comparing aggressive young males with primates in the jungle, and the violence initiative died in the resulting furor. But even to be proposing such a biomedical approach to criminal justice shows how far the intellectual pendulum has swung toward biology.

The eugenics movement of the 1930s was fueled at least in part by a desire to get rid of habitual criminals, and many attempts have been made over the years to identify genetic roots for aggression, violence, and criminality. A 1965 study, for instance, found that imprisoned criminals were more likely than other people to have an extra Y chromosome (and therefore more male genes). The evidence linking this chromosomal aberration to crime was skimpy and tenuous, but politics often runs ahead of the evidence: Soon after, a Boston hospital actually started screening babies for the defect, the idea being to intervene early with counseling should personality problems become apparent. The screening was halted when further study showed that XYY men, while slightly less intelligent, were not unusually aggressive.

As with many psychopathologies, criminal aggression is difficult to define precisely for research. Indeed, crime and alcohol abuse are so entangled that it's often difficult to know whether genetic markers are associated with drinking, criminality—or something else entirely, like a personality trait. A 1993 National Research Council study, for example, reported strong evidence of genetic influence on antisocial personality disorder, but it also noted that many genes are probably involved.

...

Mutations and Emotions

Just two decades ago, the National Institute of Mental Health was funding studies of economic recession, unemployment, and urban ills as possible contributors to serious emotional disturbance. A whole branch of psychiatry known as "social psychiatry" was dedicated to helping the mentally ill by rooting out such pathogens as poverty and racism. There is no longer much evidence of these sensibilities at work today. NIMH now focuses its studies almost exclusively on brain research and on the genetic underpinnings of emotional illnesses.

The decision to reorder the federal research portfolio was both scientific and political. Major advances in neuroscience methods opened up research that wasn't possible a generation ago, and that research has paid off in drugs that very effectively treat some disorders. But there was also a concerted political campaign to reinterpret mental illness. A generation ago, the leading theory about schizophrenia was that this devastating emotional and mental disorder was caused by cold and distant mothering, itself the result of the mother's unconscious wish that her child had never been born. A nationwide lobbying effort was launched to combat such unfounded mother blaming, and 20 years later that artifact of the Freudian era is entirely discredited. It's widely accepted today that psychotic disorders are brain disorders, probably with genetic roots.

Besotted Genes

The best that can be said about research on the genetics of alcoholism is that it's inconclusive, but that hasn't stopped people from using genetic arguments for political purposes. The disease model for alcoholism is practically a secular religion in this country, embraced by psychiatry, most treatment clinics, and (perhaps most important) by Alcoholics Anonymous. What this means is that those seeking help for excessive drinking are told they have a disease (though the exact nature of the disease is unknown), that it's probably a genetic condition, and that the only treatment is abstinence.

But the evidence is not strong enough to support these claims. There are several theories of how genes might lead to excessive drinking. A genetic insensitivity to alcohol, for example, might cause certain people to drink more; or alcoholics might metabolize alcohol differently; or they may have inherited a certain personality type that's prone to risk-taking or stimulus-seeking. While studies of family pedigrees and adoptees have on occasion indicated a familial pattern for a particular form of alcoholism (early-onset disorder in men, for example), just as often they reveal no pattern. This shouldn't be all that surprising, given the difficulty of defining alcoholism. Some researchers identify alcoholics by their drunk-driving record, while others focus on withdrawal symptoms or daily consumption. This is what geneticists call a "dirty phenotype"; people drink too much in so many different ways that the trait itself is hard to define, so family patterns are all over the place, and often contradictory.

Given these methodological problems, researchers have been trying to locate an actual gene (or genes) that might be involved in alcoholism. A 1990 study reported that a severe form of the disorder (most of the subjects in the study had cirrhosis of the liver) was linked to a gene that codes for a chemical receptor for the neurotransmitter dopamine. The researchers even developed and patented a test for the genetic mutation, but subsequent attempts to confirm the dopamine connection have failed.

The issues of choice and responsibility come up again and again in discussions of alcoholism and other addictive disorders. Even if scientists were to identify a gene (or genes) that create a susceptibility to alcoholism, it's hard to know what this genetic "loading" would mean. It certainly wouldn't lead to alcoholism in a culture that didn't condone drinking—among the Amish, for example—so it's not deterministic in a strict sense. Even in a culture where drinking is common, there are clearly a lot of complicated choices involved in living an alcoholic life; it's difficult to make the leap from DNA to those choices. While few would want to return to the time when heavy drinking was condemned as strictly a moral failing or character flaw, many are concerned that the widely accepted disease model of alcoholism actually provides people with an excuse for their destructive behavior....

Synapses of Desire

It would be a mistake to focus only on biological explanations of psychopathology; the cultural shift is much broader than that. A generation ago, the gay community was at war with organized psychiatry, arguing (successfully) that sexual orientation was a lifestyle choice and ought to be deleted from the manual of disorders. Recently the same community was celebrating new evidence that homosexuality is a biological (and perhaps genetic) trait, not a choice at all.

Three lines of evidence support the idea of a genetic basis for homosexuality, none of them conclusive. A study of twins and adopted siblings found that about half of identical twins of homosexual men were themselves gay, compared with 22 percent of fraternal twins and 11 percent of adoptees; a similar pattern was found among women. While such a pattern is consistent with some kind of genetic loading for sexual orientation, critics contend it also could be explained by the very similar experiences many twins share. And, of course, half the identical twins did not become gay—which by definition means something other than genes must be involved.

...

The only study so far to report an actual genetic connection to homosexuality is a 1993 study by Dean Hamer, a National Institutes of Health biologist who identified a genetic marker on the X chromosome in 75 percent of gay brothers. The functional significance of this piece of DNA is unknown, and subsequent research has not succeeded in duplicating Hamer's results.

Homosexuality represents a bit of a paradox when it comes to the intertwined issues of choice and determinism. When Hamer reported his genetic findings, many in the gay community celebrated, believing that society would be more tolerant of behavior rooted in biology and DNA rather than choice.... [I]n a strange twist, liberals found themselves arguing the deterministic position, while conservatives insisted that homosexuality is a choice. The argument of gay-rights advocates was that biological status conveyed legal status—and protection under the law.

History's Warning

But history suggests otherwise.... During the eugenics movement of the 1920s and 1930s, both in the United States and Europe, society became less, not more, tolerant of human variation and misfortune. Based on racial theories that held Eastern Europeans to be genetically inferior to Anglo-Saxon stock, Congress passed (and Calvin Coolidge signed) a 1924 law to restrict immigration, and by 1940 more than 30 states had laws permitting forced sterilization of people suffering from such conditions as "feeblemindedness," pauperism, and mental illness. The ultimate outcome of the eugenics craze in Europe is well known; homosexuals were not given extra sympathy or protection in the Third Reich's passion to purify genetic stock.

...

More and more experts, including dedicated biologists, sense that the power of genetics has been oversold and that a correction is needed. What's more, there's a glimmer of evidence that the typical American may not be buying it entirely. According to a recent ... poll, less than one American in five believes that genes play a major role in controlling behavior; three-quarters cite environment and society as the more powerful shapers of our lives. Whether the behavior under question is a disorder like addiction, mental illness, or violence, or a trait like homosexuality, most believe that heredity plays some role, but not a primary one. Indeed, 40 percent think genes play no role whatsoever in homosexuality, and a similar percentage think heredity is irrelevant to drug addiction and criminality. Across the board, most believe that people's lives are shaped by the choices they make.

...

Whatever's going on, it's clear that this new mistrust of genetic power is consonant with what science is now beginning to show. Indeed, the very expression "gene for" is misleading.... [W]hen geneticists say they've found a gene for a particular trait, what they mean is that people carrying a certain "allele"—a variation in a stretch of DNA that normally codes for a certain protein—will develop the given trait in a standard environment. The last few words—"in a standard environment"—are very important, because what scientists are not saying is that a given allele will necessarily lead to that trait in every environment. Indeed, there is mounting evidence that a particular allele will not produce the same result if the environment changes significantly; that is to say, the environment has a strong influence on whether and how a gene gets "expressed."

It's hard to emphasize too much what a radical rethinking of the nature-nurture debate this represents. When most people think about heredity, they still think in terms of classical Mendelian genetics: one gene, one trait. But for most complex human behaviors, this is far from the reality that recent research is revealing. A more accurate view very likely involves many different genes, some of which control other genes, and many of which are controlled by signals from the environment. To complicate matters further, the

environment is very complicated in itself, ranging from the things we typically lump under nurture (parenting, family dynamics, schooling, safe housing) to biological encounters like viruses and birth complications, even
biochemical events within cells.

The relative contributions of genes and the environment are not addi-
tive, as in such-and-such a percentage of nature, such-and-such a percentage of experience; that's the old view, no longer credited. Nor is it true that
full genetic expression happens once, around birth, after which we take our
genetic legacy into the world to see how far it gets us. Genes produce proteins
throughout the lifespan, in many different environments, or they don't produce those proteins, depending on how rich or harsh or impoverished those
environments are....

The emerging view of nature-nurture is that many complicated behaviors probably have some measure of genetic loading that gives some people
a susceptibility—for schizophrenia, for instance, or for aggression. But the
development of the behavior or pathology requires more, what National Institute of Mental Health Director Stephen Hyman calls an environmental
"second hit." This second hit operates, counterintuitively, through the genes
themselves to "sculpt" the brain. So with depression, for example, it appears
as though a bad experience in the world—for example, a devastating loss—
can actually create chemical changes in the body that affect certain genes,
which in turn affect certain brain proteins that make a person more suscep-
tible to depression in the future. Nature or nurture? Similarly, Hyman's own
work has shown that exposure to addictive substances can lead to biochemical changes at the genetic and molecular levels that commandeer brain cir-
cuits involving volition—and thus undermine the very motivation needed
to take charge of one's destructive behavior. So the choice to experiment with
drugs or alcohol may, in certain people, create the biological substrate of the
addictive disorder. The distinction between biology and experience begins to
lose its edge.

Nurturing Potentials

Just as bad experiences can turn on certain vulnerability genes, rich and challenging experiences have the power to enhance life, again acting through
the genes. Greenough has shown in rat studies that by providing cages full
of toys and complex structures that are continually rearranged—"the animal
equivalent of Head Start"—he can increase the number of synapses in the
rats' brains by 25 percent and blood flow by 85 percent. Talent and intelligence
appear extraordinarily malleable.

Child-development experts refer to the life circumstances that enhance (or undermine) gene expression as "proximal processes," a term
coined by psychologist Urie Bronfenbrenner. Everything from lively con-
versation to games to the reading of stories can potentially get a gene to

turn on and create a protein that may become a neuronal receptor or messenger chemical involved in thinking or mood. "No genetic potential can become reality," says Bronfenbrenner, "unless the relationship between the organism and its environment is such that it is permitted to be expressed." Unfortunately, as he details in his new book, *The State of Americans*, the circumstances in which many American children are living are becoming more impoverished year by year.

If there's a refrain among geneticists working today, it's this: The harder we work to demonstrate the power of heredity, the harder it is to escape the potency of experience. It's a bit paradoxical, because in a sense we end up once again with the old pre-1950s paradigm, but arrived at with infinitely more sophisticated tools: Yes, the way to intervene in human lives and improve them, to ameliorate mental illness, addictions, and criminal behavior, is to enrich impoverished environments, to improve conditions in the family and society. What's changed is that the argument is coming not from left-leaning sociologists, but from those most intimate with the workings of the human genome. The goal of psychosocial interventions is optimal gene expression.

So assume for a minute that there is a cluster of genes somehow associated with youthful violence. The kid who carries those genes might inhabit a world of loving parents, regular nutritious meals, lots of books, safe schools. Or his world might be a world of peeling paint and gunshots around the corner. In which environment would those genes be likely to manufacture the biochemical underpinnings of criminality? Or for that matter, the proteins and synapses of happiness?

KEY WEBSITES

DEFINING THE DEFECTIVE: MASS CULTURE AND THE MEANINGS OF HEREDITARY DISEASE IN AMERICAN EUGENICS

Martin S. Pernick, "Defining the Defective: Mass Culture and the Meanings of Hereditary Disease in American Eugenics": At its peak in the 1910s and 1920s, the scientific movement known as eugenics helped initiate a sweeping range of activities intended to "improve human heredity" and eliminate hereditary disabilities. In the United States, eugenically sponsored measures included advanced statistical analyses of human pedigrees, "better baby contests" modeled on rural livestock shows, compulsory sterilization of criminals and the disabled, and selective ethnic restrictions on immigration. But before eugenics could implement such methods for improving heredity, it needed to diagnose who was hereditarily "fit" and who was "defective." The construction of these diagnostic distinctions, what was meant by "improvement" and what was meant by "hereditary," is the subject of this paper.
http://www.stanford.edu/class/history133/Pernick/Pernick_ Defining_Defective.html

EUGENICS: THE SCIENCE OF BREEDING MEN

W. I. Thomas, "Eugenics: The Science of Breeding Men," *American Magazine* 68 (1909): 190–197: W. I. Thomas is one of the founders of sociology. Here is a paper he wrote in 1909 in which he extols the virtues of eugenics. As he notes, "Eugenics must join with the other branches of sociology, and with economics, medicine, civics, and education in the development of sentiments and measures for the better nurture of children. And when this is done much that is positively bad and threatening in society will disappear. On the side of selective reproduction it will have to develop a program answering to all the social facts and to the facts of heredity. In addition it will have to develop a sentiment for those marriages which have good reproduction in view. It is thought by some that the development of this latter sentiment will be difficult or impossible, owing to the unwillingness of the young people to act on other than sentimental and romantic impulses in marriage. But the history of society shows fortunately that there is no sentiment too difficult for introduction and acceptance."
http://paradigm.soci.brocku.ca/~lward/Thomas/Thomas_22.html

NOT GUILTY, BY REASON OF GENETIC DETERMINISM

Mark Philpott, "Not Guilty, by Reason of Genetic Determinism": The possibility that genetic research might identify 'genes for criminal tendencies' has stimulated intense controversy. News coverage of a conference in London in

1995 on "The Genetics of Criminal and Antisocial Behavior" brought the question of a link between genetics and criminal behavior to wide public attention. Since then a steady output of newspaper articles and television documentaries has reflected continuing interest and concern over the suggestion that criminals might be born, not made. The nature/nurture debate rages on in many channels, but among psychologists and geneticists it is largely resolved: Both are important. In this paper, Philpott examines *Weak Genetic Determinism* (genetics has a role in the causation of a range of behavioral and/or personality traits relevant to criminality) and *Strong Genetic Determinism* (genetics is a causally sufficient condition, under normal circumstances, for a range of behavioral and/or personality traits that lead to criminality).

**http://www.med.upenn.edu/~bioethic/genetics/articles/4.philpott
.not.guilty.html**

GENETICS AND THE CONTROL OF CRIME

Tabitha M. Powledge, "Genetics and the Control of Crime": Powledge notes that genetics is unlikely to contribute significantly to reducing or preventing crime. In short, crime is never going to be very big in the genetics business, and genetics is never going to be very big in the crime business. It is not simply that scientists lack facts about the relation of DNA to crime (with, to be sure, one noteworthy exception: More than 80 percent of those arrested for any crime, and more than 90 percent of those arrested for violent crime, possess a Y chromosome). Nor is it just that ignorance renders it premature to incorporate genetics into crime policy. The difficulty is considerably more basic. The more that is learned, the clearer it becomes that the knowledge gained is unlikely to generate practical strategies for dealing with that motley mass of disparate actions—ranging from stock fraud to serial homicide—we lump under the catchall rubric of crime.

http://www.aibs.org/biosciencelibrary/vol46/jan.96.crime.html

BIOETHICS.NET

Bioethics.net is produced and supported by the Center for Bioethics at the University of Pennsylvania. It is the Internet's first and largest site on bioethics and addresses social, medical, and research issues. The content is appropriate for both novices and experts. The center's mission "is to advance scholarly and public understanding of ethical, legal, social, and public policy issues in health care." The goal is to bring ethical issues and modern technology to the people.

http://www.med.upenn.edu/~bioethic/index.shtml

Do We Need More Gun Control Laws?

Those who oppose gun control claim the Second Amendment to the Constitution guarantees them the right to own guns. So what does the Second Amendment say? The Second Amendment says, "A well regulated militia being necessary to the security of a free state, the right of the people to keep and bear arms shall not be infringed."

This curious syntax has perplexed most modern readers: How do the two main clauses with different subject-nouns fit together? Do these words guarantee a right of militias, as the first clause seems to suggest, or a right of people, as the second clause seems to say? In one corner, gun controllers embrace a narrow reading, insisting that the amendment merely confers a right on state governments to establish professional state militias like the National Guard or local swat teams. No ordinary citizen is covered by the amendment in this view.

In the other corner, gun owners and their supporters read the amendment in a broad, libertarian way, arguing that it protects a right of every individual to have guns for self-protection, for hunting, or collecting. Virtually nothing having to do with personal weaponry is outside the amendment in this view.

Gun control advocates believe the proliferation of guns in this country is responsible for an increase in the violent crime rate. Those opposed to gun control acknowledge that there is a great deal of gun-related violent crime in this country, including homicide, robbery, and assault. They also admit that there has been a proliferation of firearms in this country that has been steadily increasing. But they dispute the argument that this is a result of there being too many guns available to people. Gun control opponents claim that violence is not related to how many guns there are in a given population; it instead depends on how they are distributed in that population—that is, who has them and for what purpose. Gun-control laws characteristically ignore that distinction, and usually aim only to limit the number of weapons in circulation.

Those opposed to gun control believe that comparing the United States to the low guns/low crime societies of the United Kingdom or Canada is one of the most common mistakes gun control advocates make. Gun control opponents point out that there are countries with every permutation: the United States (high guns/high crime); Switzerland and Israel (high guns/low crime); Japan (low guns/low crime); and Mexico (low guns/high crime). Any two countries can be compared or contrasted to make any point desired.

Gun control advocates claim that it is not so much that guns "cause" crime as that they cause the outcomes of whatever crimes there are to be more deadly. The claim has a basis in common sense. It is reasonable to think that a certain number of intentional killings would be unfeasible without a gun. And many killings develop out of a domestic brawl or an argument between neighbors and not a specific intention to kill. Murder resulted simply because a gun was handy; without a gun the offender would have used a chair or a knife, and his victim in all probability would have lived. Although gun control may not make people any less violent or reduce how often they come into conflict with one another, it could at least make it less likely that a given conflict becomes a fatal one. Therefore, lives would be saved if some aggressors could be denied guns.

Gun control opponents claim gun laws burden only the law-abiding citizen. They also claim that gun laws do not work—or more specifically, that they cannot be used to keep guns out of the hands of criminals. Gun control advocates believe these are myths, and the longer they are kept alive, the more difficult it is to reduce the amount of crime and criminal violence that occurs in the United States. They note that well-tailored gun laws work. The Brady Law is working to prevent easy access to handguns by criminals. Since the law was first implemented, eighty-five felons a day have been denied access to a handgun that they tried to purchase from licensed gun dealers.

Douglas Weil presents many of the gun control arguments in "Gun Control Laws Can Reduce Crime." He notes that most studies support the notion that well-tailored gun laws can have a beneficial impact on gun violence, while laws that indiscriminately increase access to firearms may have the opposite effect. For example, researchers found a "prompt decline in homicides and suicides by firearms in the District of Columbia" following implementation of a restrictive licensing law for handguns in the District. Conversely, the evidence from the five urban areas studied suggests that relaxing restrictions on carrying concealed firearms led to an increase in gun homicides.

Gary Kleck disagrees, and, in "Struggling against 'Common Sense': The Pluses and Minuses of Gun Control," points out that the defensive use of guns is common—far more common than criminal use—and is effective in preventing injury and the completion of crimes. Thus, the availability of guns among noncriminals has significant crime- and injury-reducing effects. He also notes that, ironically, it is the very deadliness of guns that can be responsible for reducing violence. Kleck believes that the deadliness of guns allows aggressors to get what they want without having to actually inflict injuries on their victims.

Gun Control Laws
Can Reduce Crime

Douglas Weil

Over the past few years, many state legislatures have debated, and a significant number have passed, legislation that eases restrictions on carrying concealed handguns. At the heart of this effort is the belief that "encouraging gun ownership might be a partial solution to the crime problem."

The evidence that crime reduction can be achieved through the proliferation of gun ownership and gun carrying is weak, and the strategy is dangerous because it is based on the false premise that acquiring a firearm for protection will, in general, make people safer.

...

There is, of course, a sensible alternative to those who envision America as a place in which the citizenry is responsible for combating crime by arming itself. The alternative is to: (1) put into place a well-tailored, comprehensive set of gun control measures designed to disrupt the illegal trafficking and distribution of firearms, and (2) apply appropriate pressure to the gun industry to ensure that the design and marketing strategies for firearms that are brought to the market minimize the potential for criminal use of guns while respecting the legitimate use of these weapons.

The use of a gun for protection is an incredibly rare event—a fact that simply won't change if more people are "armed and dangerous." But bringing more guns into homes—where married couples occasionally fight, in which teens sometimes contemplate suicide, and in which the curiosity of young children often leads them to look through their parents' dresser drawers—will lead to more death. Rather than enabling their citizens to carry concealed guns into movie theaters, shopping malls, and grocery stores, other

From *The World & I* (February 1, 1997). Copyright © 1997. Reprinted with the permission of *The World & I*, a publication of The Washington Times Corporation.

industrialized nations have enacted laws that curb the supply of handguns to criminals and other individuals who pose a high risk to society. In 1992, there were 13,220 handgun murders in the United States; Great Britain had 33. Isn't it obvious that there is a better way?

Faulty Research Perpetuates Myths

...

Twice each year, the federal government obtains data on the frequency, characteristics, and consequences of criminal victimization from a nationally representative sample of fifty thousand households that participate in the National Crime Victimization Survey. It is the best available data on criminal victimization in the country. Researchers at the University of Maryland analyzed these data and concluded that "criminals face little threat from armed victims." Though the researchers estimated that victims use firearms for protection approximately 65,000 times a year, they concluded that when "coupled with the risks of keeping a gun in the home for protection, these results raise questions about the collective benefits of civilian firearm ownership for crime control."

...

More to the point, if carrying a concealed handgun were going to have a beneficial impact on crime, the deterrent effect would, presumably, be related to predatory crimes between strangers that occur on the street. Consequently, easing restrictions on the carrying of concealed weapons should have the biggest impact on robbery. Fewer than one in five murders occur in connection with a predatory crime, and the majority of rapes and aggravated assaults occur between people who know each other—and they often occur in the home. Robbery typically occurs on the street and between strangers.

...

[R]esearchers have concluded that there is no beneficial impact on crime associated with easing restrictions on carrying concealed handguns. In fact, in a study of five large urban areas, researchers at the University of Maryland concluded that easing restrictions on carrying concealed weapons was associated with an increase in gun-related murders that was not offset by a decrease in murders committed with other weapons. The researchers hypothesized that criminals responded to the change in the law by arming themselves more frequently, doing so with more powerful weapons, and being quicker to use their guns during the commission of a crime.

Gun Laws Work

There is little published research on the effectiveness of gun laws, though with little dissent, most of the studies that do exist support the notion that well-tailored gun laws can have a beneficial impact on gun violence, while laws that indiscriminately increase access to firearms may have the opposite effect. For example, researchers found a "prompt decline in homicides and suicides by firearms in the District of Columbia" following implementation of a restrictive licensing law for handguns in the District. Conversely, the evidence from the five urban areas studied suggests that relaxing restrictions on carrying concealed firearms led to an increase in gun homicides.

Researchers have also shown that we have effective strategies for disrupting the illegal interstate trafficking of firearms. In July 1993, Virginia became the second state in the nation to limit handgun purchases by individuals to one gun a month (though gun collectors can obtain permission to exceed the legal limit). Prior to the enactment of the law, individuals were able to purchase an unlimited number of handguns from licensed dealers as part of a single transaction. The law was passed because Virginia was a principal supplier of guns to the illegal market, particularly to the northeastern part of the United States. In fact, prior to the law, 35 percent of all guns that were originally obtained in the Southeast and then illegally trafficked to New York, New Jersey, Connecticut, Rhode Island, or Massachusetts came from Virginia. Shortly after the law took effect, the percentage of guns that were being trafficked to the Northeast from Virginia fell to only 16 percent.

The truth is that crime and the violent outcomes associated with criminal activity are affected by a variety of factors, and society's response cannot be monolithic or simplistic. Part of the solution is implementation of a comprehensive set of well-tailored gun laws directed at keeping guns out of the illegal market. In 1993, 1.1 million violent crimes were committed with handguns—many of which were acquired in the illegal market. In fact, when asked, approximately 30 to 43 percent of criminals identify the illegal market as the source of their last handgun.

The illegal market exists for a variety of reasons. Would-be criminals may be unable to buy handguns from the legal market, because a prior criminal record disqualifies them from legally purchasing the weapons. To date, because of the Brady Law, more than 100,000 prohibited purchasers (including 72,000 felons) were denied access to a handgun that they attempted to purchase from a gun dealer. Others may go to the illegal market because they want to make it difficult for law enforcement to trace a gun back to them—something that can also be accomplished by purchasing a gun from the private or secondary market (transactions that do not involve a licensed gun dealer). The ability to acquire guns from the illegal or the secondary market points to one of the most troubling aspects of society's attempts to prevent gun violence—the ease with which the link between a gun and the individual who uses it can be broken, removing an important impediment to the criminal use of firearms.

In many jurisdictions, identification requirements for the purchase of a firearm are minimal and easily falsified, while private or secondary market sales are largely unregulated. A prohibited purchaser or individual who, for any reason, does not want to be identified as the owner of a particular gun can obtain a firearm directly from the secondary market with little risk of being stopped or identified. Alternatively, the same individual could recruit a third party (known as a "straw purchaser") to buy the gun in his place. If a gun bought by a straw purchaser turns up as part of a criminal investigation, the straw purchaser can, with little risk of criminal culpability, claim that he sold the firearm to an unidentifiable third party.

To make it more difficult to break the link between a gun and the individual who uses it—and therefore to reduce the supply of guns available to criminals, several steps can be taken:

- Individuals should be required to obtain a license (or "permit-to-purchase") before being allowed to buy a gun, particularly a handgun. The license should be issued only after the applicant provides proof of residency and submits to a fingerprint-based background check.
- All handgun transfers (if not all firearms transfers) should be registered.
- Laws that regulate the purchase of a firearm from a licensed gun dealer should be extended to private, secondary market transactions.
- Handgun purchases should be limited to one gun every thirty days.

Taken together, these measures will make it more difficult for gun traffickers to supply the illegal market with firearms. Also, requiring individuals to obtain a license prior to purchasing a firearm will make it more difficult to purchase a gun using false identification. As a result, there will be a greater need for individuals who do not want their names associated with the purchase of a gun to seek out straw purchasers to buy the gun for them, though recruiting straw purchasers should be more difficult. Fewer individuals would be willing to act as straw purchasers if they were required to submit their names to law enforcement for a background check to buy a gun that they intend to illegally transfer to a third party.

Requiring that all firearms transfers be registered, including those in the private market, would likely further complicate the process of recruiting straw purchasers. If all transfers are registered, then the most recent owner of a gun recovered as part of a criminal investigation can be easily identified, and when asked, that individual will not be free to say that he passed the gun on to an unidentifiable third party. Because registration has the potential to make it difficult for an individual to break the link between his possession and use of a firearm, the California Police Chiefs Association has called for registration of all handgun transfers.

...

The Gun Industry Needs to Take Responsibility

Well-tailored gun laws should be a part of society's response to crime and the violence associated with criminal activity, but it should not be the only response. The gun industry, through its own actions in the development of products it brings to the market, contributes to the problems society faces. Consequently, the industry should be pressured to take responsibility for its contribution to the problem in the hope that it can be part of the solution.

The gun industry manufactures and markets the only widely available consumer products designed to kill. As designed, however, most guns can be fired by virtually anyone who gains access to them—whether a three-year-old child or an unauthorized adult who steals a gun and then uses it to commit other crimes. But guns could be designed differently. Readily available technology exists that can be used to "personalize" guns so that they can be fired only by authorized users. The industry, however, has failed to incorporate this technology into the design of its products while producing an endless stream of products better suited to criminal purposes than legitimate use.

Gun manufacturers, for example, have brought to the market assault pistols that accept silencers and high-capacity ammunition magazines along with low-quality, easily concealable "Saturday Night Specials." More recently, the industry has developed ever smaller versions of its high-powered 9mm semiautomatic pistols. Without a doubt, the gun industry is able to innovate new designs of its lethal products—it just chooses to innovate for death and injury rather than for safety. Like the tobacco industry, the gun industry must accept the burden of responsibility for preventing the criminal and violent outcomes associated with the use of the products they design and sell.

Conclusion

A number of myths are associated with gun control. One of these myths is that gun laws burden only the law-abiding citizen. Another myth is that gun laws do not work—or more specifically, that they cannot be used to keep guns out of the hands of criminals. But these are clearly myths, and the longer they are kept alive, the more difficult it is to make rational decisions about the proper role of gun control in the broader effort to reduce the amount of crime and criminal violence that occurs in the United States.

We know that well-tailored gun laws work. The Brady Law is working to prevent easy access to handguns by criminals. Since the law was first implemented, 85 felons a day have been denied access to a handgun that they tried to purchase from licensed gun dealers. Virginia's law limiting handgun purchases to one gun a month has had an enormous impact on gun trafficking patterns along the East Coast. This law should be extended to cover handgun purchases in all states. Who besides gun traffickers need to be allowed to purchase more than one handgun every thirty days?

Most gun control policies currently advocated in the United States (e.g., licensing, registration, regulation of secondary market sales, and one gun a month) could be best described as efforts to limit the supply of guns to the illegal market, and the tools necessary to maintain the link between the guns that are used for illegal purposes and the criminals who have used them. And they should be part of a rational strategy to reduce gun violence in America.

The gun lobby believes an armed society is a polite society—"much social order in America may depend on the fact that millions of people are armed and dangerous to each other." Well, America is an armed society (a firearm can be found in 40 percent of all households in the United States), but it is difficult to say that our tremendous firepower has made us safe.

It is time to try a better way. It is time to make a serious effort to keep guns out of the hands of criminals. And it is time for the gun industry to became a partner in the effort to reduce the level of violence caused by the products it brings to the market. We need to implement a comprehensive set of gun laws designed to limit the number of guns available to criminals.

Struggling against "Common Sense": The Pluses and Minuses of Gun Control

Gary Kleck

It is not hard to persuade people that your position on an issue is correct when they have no opinion on the issue to begin with. It is considerably harder to change well-established views, and very hard indeed to change what people regard as "common sense." Such is the case with the debate over gun control. Enlightened thinking among the nation's opinion-molding elite holds to the simple view that where weapons are more common, there is bound to be more violence. Conversely, if gun control can reduce the number of weapons, there will be fewer violent deaths.

Unfortunately, "common sense" often refers to ideas to which we are so firmly committed that we will not reconsider them even in light of new information. We consider them to be so obviously true that a reevaluation would be a waste of time. Of course, it was once equally obvious that the earth was flat and that the sun moved around a fixed earth.

The Argument for Gun Control

The standard rationale in favor of gun control, when any coherent rationale at all is offered, goes something like this: Although gun control may not make people any less violent or reduce how often they come into conflict with one another, it could at least make it less likely that a given conflict becomes a fatal one. Aggressors denied a gun might well seek a substitute like a knife, but an attack with a knife is much less likely to be fatal than one with a gun. Therefore, lives would be saved if some aggressors could be denied guns.

From *The World & I* (February 1, 1997). Copyright © 1997. Reprinted with the permission of *The World & I*, a publication of The Washington Times Corporation.

This argument works only if one makes many dubious but unstated assumptions. First, those making the argument assume that the observed difference in fatality rates between gunshot woundings and knife woundings is entirely or largely due to the difference in weapons. However, even pro-control experts ... have conceded that people tend to choose tools that are suited to their tasks, and that those with more lethal intentions are likely to choose more lethal tools. Thus, at least part of the observed difference in fatality rates between gun and knife woundings is due to people differences rather than weapon differences. The implication is that even though the difference in fatality rates between guns and knives might be four to one, getting rid of guns would not reduce the fatality rate of assaults to one-fourth its current level, since the greater lethality of aggressors who would have used guns would not be altered by denying them guns.

The Costs of Limiting Controls to Handguns

Another key assumption underlying pro-control argumentation, largely dictated by political realities, is that the controls that would disarm aggressors and thereby save lives are handgun controls. Indeed, the vast majority of both existing and proposed controls are either exclusively aimed at handguns or impose stricter controls on handguns than on other common types of guns such as shotguns and rifles. Since there is more public support for handgun controls, and handguns are involved in roughly four of every five gun crimes, this focus seems perfectly reasonable.

Once the debate is focused on handguns, however, the "substitution" issue changes in a significant way. Assuming we succeeded in making handguns unavailable, to at least some would-be criminals, the remaining weapon choice would not be guns versus knives or other nongun weapons. Rather, the choice for handgun-deprived criminals would be between nongun weapons (knives, clubs, etc.) and the relatively unregulated long guns (i.e., shotguns and rifles).

The obvious problem with passing laws that create this set of options is that long guns are substantially more lethal than handguns. Indeed, the difference in lethality between long guns and handguns may well be as great as that between guns and knives. Inducing criminals who would otherwise have used handguns to use long guns instead is tantamount to encouraging them to upgrade their weapons to more lethal substitutes. This would result in a higher share of gun-attack victims dying, among those whose attackers substituted long guns.

To be sure, some handgun crimes are committed in circumstances where only a small concealable weapon like a handgun could be used. This, however, is the exception rather than the rule. Most gun homicides are committed in either of two situations: (1) They are unplanned but occur in a private location, such as the attacker's home, where the gun is already available and where concealability is irrelevant, or (2) they are the result of planning, either of the killing itself or some other crime like a robbery that led to the killing. Those who committed their crimes in or near their own homes, such as domestic-violence offenders, would not need a concealable weapon. And those who planned their crimes could easily make a shotgun sufficiently small to conceal under a sports jacket or raincoat by devoting five minutes with a hacksaw to shortening the gun's barrel and stock.

Given that many long guns are as cheap as the average handgun and even more widely available, why would most prospective killers not substitute a more lethal long gun? Surveys of imprisoned felons have asked what they would do if they wanted to carry a handgun but could not get one. Nearly three-quarters of the gun criminals indicated that they would carry a sawed-off long gun instead.

Consequently, the guns-versus-knives substitution argument is something of a red herring in a legislative context where "gun control" is really mostly handgun control. The key issue is not one of legal controls inducing aggressors to substitute less-lethal weapons, but rather one of inadvertently inducing the substitution of more-lethal ones.

...

How Do Guns Affect Violence?

Although the answers might seem self-evident to some readers, it is worth going into why we would want to control guns. How does the availability of firearms affect the level of violence in America, assuming it does at all? The standard pro-control rationale is correct with respect to one way guns can affect violence: Victims wounded by a gunshot are indeed more likely to die than those wounded with knives or other weapons. Guns are more lethal than other weapons commonly used in assaults—perhaps two or three times as deadly as knives.

This crucial fact, however, does not have exclusively violence-increasing implications. Ironically, it is the very deadliness of guns that is responsible for certain violence-reducing effects as well. The violence-reducing effects of victims using guns defensively come to mind easily, and these will be discussed later. However, even guns in the hands of aggressors can have violence-reducing effects. The deadliness of guns allows aggressors to get what they want without having to actually inflict injuries on their victims. For example, robbers armed with guns can, and usually do, intimidate their victims into relinquishing their property without attacking the victim, while unarmed robbers typically open the encounter by hurting the victim. Likewise, assault-minded aggressors who are angry at someone can terrify, dominate, or humiliate their victims by pointing a gun at them, while those without deadly weapons have to actually injure their victims to achieve these emotional goals.

In short, guns often serve as a substitute for attack, rather than a means of attack. It is ironic that so many people are unwilling to accept this conclusion when empirical evidence is unanimously supportive. Every single one of seventeen studies known to me that have compared aggressors with guns and those without guns has found that those with guns are less likely to attack and injure their victims.

In sum, while aggressors with guns are more likely to kill if they do hurt their victims, they are also less likely to hurt them in the first place. Both of these effects are important, but it should be noted that 97 percent of violent crimes committed by offenders with guns do not involve any gunshot wounds being inflicted on the victim. This means that, in 97 percent of gun crimes, exactly how lethal gunshot wounds are relative to other weapons is irrelevant to whether the victim will die—in crimes where the victim is not shot at all, it is obviously impossible for the victim to die of a gunshot wound.

In these 97 percent of the cases, therefore, the dominant effect of the aggressor having a gun is to make it less likely the victim will be hurt. In the other 3 percent of the cases, the aggressor's use of a gun increases the probability that the wound inflicted will be fatal. This raises the possibility that the net effect of these two phenomena combined with the likelihood of the victim being killed could be zero. Consequently, it is not obvious that even gun possession among criminals has a net homicide-increasing effect.

...

Consequently, gun controls that effectively disarm crime-prone persons could reduce the rate at which attacks and robberies are attempted in the first place, even if they did not reduce the share of such crimes that result in a victim's death.

Guns in the Hands of Crime Victims

The pro-control argument implicitly assumes that the aggressor is the only party to a violent crime who is likely to have a gun. The assumption is obviously true only some of the time. If it is often the victim who is the one with the gun, and victims use their guns to reduce their chances of injury, then prohibitionist laws making guns scarce could make things worse by reducing the number of victims who are able to effectively protect themselves.

Whether applied to all guns, a broad subcategory like handguns, or a small subset such as those guns labeled assault weapons, prohibitionist controls all share the common trait of being aimed at denying guns to both criminals and noncriminals alike. In contrast to regulatory measures such as background checks, which are aimed at denying guns to only members of high-risk groups such as those with prior criminal convictions, prohibitionist measures theoretically apply with equal force to criminals and noncriminals, would-be offenders and prospective victims.

In practice, however, actual compliance with bans is not likely to be equal among criminals and noncriminals. By definition, the law-abiding are more likely to obey laws, including gun control laws, than are lawbreakers. Thus, prohibitionist measures in general, regardless of how many criminals they may disarm, will almost certainly disarm noncriminals at an even higher rate.

If there were no cost to disarming noncriminals, this would be relatively inconsequential, except with respect to recreational uses of guns, and using prohibitionist measures to disarm criminals therefore might make sense. Unfortunately, there are very serious costs.

...

For a long time, it was thought that self-defense with a gun was both rare and ineffective. Those who attempted such a thing were branded fools by self-appointed "experts" among police chiefs and academics. It was commonly claimed, with nothing more than anecdotal (and possibly apocryphal) supporting evidence, that trying to use a gun for protection would only provoke a criminal into hurting the victim. Worse still, victims were likely, it was alleged, to have the gun taken away and used against them.

To be sure, there have been at least a few real-world incidents where these sorts of things have happened. For the most part, however, these purported risks are myths. I have examined the largest nationally representative samples of crimes in which victims used guns for self-protection. Victims using guns had their weapons taken from them by the offender in less than 1 percent of the cases. Further, victims using guns are less likely to be hurt than victims resisting in other ways. Indeed, those using guns are even less likely to be hurt than victims not resisting at all. For example, analysis of robberies indicates that 17 percent of victims who resisted with a gun were injured, compared with 25 percent of those who did not resist at all and 38 percent of those who used other means of resistance.

Even the 17 percent injury rate exaggerates the likelihood that gun resistance provokes robbers to hurt their victims. About two-thirds of these crimes involved robbers hurting their victims first, then the victims resisting. Injury apparently provoked resistance, rather than the reverse. At most, 6 percent of the victims using guns might have provoked the robbers into attacking them, and even this is not certain, since these few robbers might have been set on attacking the victims regardless of what they did.

Furthermore, using weapons to resist makes it less likely crimes will be completed. In rapes, this means the rapist is less likely to complete the sexual assault. In robberies, it means the robber is less likely to get away with any of the victim's property.

Resistance to the notion that armed self-defense is effective, and even relatively safe compared with other victim strategies, seems to be weakening among experts, though many nonspecialist scholars, police chiefs, policymakers, and lay people still hold to the old myths. Those scholars who now

grudgingly concede that gun resistance might sometimes be effective nevertheless fall back on a second line of defense, claiming that it is too rare to be
of any importance.

…

Those who continue to insist that such events are rare rely on a single
survey, the only source of information to ever support this view. Results from
the National Crime Victimization Survey imply only about 80,000 defensive
uses of guns each year, while fourteen other surveys all imply at least 700,000
annual uses. This grossly deviant result is apparently at least partly a product
of the victim survey's design disadvantages. It is conducted by one federal
agency, the Census Bureau, on behalf of another federal agency, the Justice
Department. It is a nonanonymous survey in which respondents are asked to
provide their address and telephone number and to divulge the names of all
household members. Given the legally ambiguous nature of many defensive
uses of guns, to report one in this survey usually requires confessing to a federal employee what might be, as far as the respondent can tell, a crime pun-
ishable by a prison term. Needless to say, this is not the ideal way to encourage
people to fully and accurately report behaviors of unknown legality. Relying
on this survey's estimate of defensive gun use frequency, while ignoring or
dismissing the results of the other fourteen surveys, is ill-informed at best, ir-
responsible at worst.

Some even sillier tactics have been adopted to support the notion that
having guns for protection is ill-advised. Repeatedly over the past twenty-
five years, reports have come out insisting that the defensive benefits of keeping guns for protection in the home are outweighed by their risks. The
measures of risk used in these reports are straightforward: counts of homicides, suicides, and fatal accidents committed with guns and occurring in the
home. The measures of defensive benefit are not so straightforward; indeed,
they are nonexistent. The only alleged "benefits" counted are justifiable homicides committed in the home with guns. Killing another human being, even
if that person was a criminal trying to victimize you, is not in any sense a
"benefit." It is a nightmare to be suffered through for years to follow. Less than
one in a thousand defensive gun uses results in a death, so counting up the
handful of defensive homicides will tell you nothing about how many times
people made good use of a gun, saved a life, prevented an injury, prevented
completion of a rape or a robbery, retained their property, or enjoyed any
other conceivable benefit.

The foolishness and futility of doing a cost-benefit analysis in which no
effort is made to measure benefit ought to be obvious to anyone. Nevertheless, citing these silly comparisons is a popular pastime, not only with members of gun control advocacy groups but also with the sort of amateur
researchers in the medical community who publish pseudoscientific articles
in medical and public health journals.

In sum, defensive use of guns is common—far more common than criminal use—and is effective in preventing injury and the completion of crimes. Thus, the availability of guns among noncriminals has significant crime-and injury-reducing effects. It is sometimes argued that, irrespective of how common or effective defensive gun use is among noncriminals, these benefits are still outweighed by the risks of gun ownership, even among noncriminals. This argument, as it pertains to noncriminals, relies on yet another dubious assumption—that serious violent acts with guns are common among otherwise noncriminal people. This assumption is crucial if one is to push for gun controls that restrict guns among noncriminals as well as criminals. The argument is that a lot of people who do violence with guns are "not really" criminals, so we need to keep guns away from everyone, including those with no prior history of violence.

...

Useful Gun Controls

Can anything worthwhile be achieved by gun control? If so, what would helpful controls look like? Research makes certain points clear about what types of controls would not work or could even be counterproductive. First, controls should be narrowly focused on making guns scarcer among high-risk subsets of the population such as persons with a prior criminal conviction, rather than being prohibitionist in character and targeting everyone. Gun bans are likely to be worse than useless because they would reduce socially useful defensive uses of guns among noncriminal victims more than they would reduce socially harmful uses by criminals. It would not just be politically unlikely and impossible in practical terms to enact prohibitionist controls. Rather, it would make things worse to try to disarm the violent minority by trying to disarm everyone or by trying to produce an overall scarcity of guns.

Second, controls should not be narrowly focused solely or primarily on handguns. Such controls encourage prospective aggressors to substitute more lethal long guns and thereby increase the share of assaults that result in the victim's death.

The main goal of a sensible weapons policy should be to make it as hard or risky as possible for high-risk individuals, such as convicted criminals, to acquire or possess guns, but without making it significantly harder for noncriminals to get them. This goal should encompass all types of guns, not just handguns, assault weapons, "Saturday Night Specials," plastic guns, or whatever else happens to be the current flavor-of-the-month in the gun control debate.

How could this be achieved? First, in those few states that do not already have such a provision, possession of all types of firearms should be banned for convicted criminals.

Second, the acquisition of all types of guns, whether through licensed dealers in stores or through private channels, should require the prospective recipient to go through an "instant records check," where a beefed-up national criminal history computer system would be used to check, within minutes, whether the person had a clean record. (The recently passed Brady Bill covers only retail transactions, currently applies only to handguns, and has constitutional problems with the way it requires states to perform the background checks for the federal government.) Existing computer coverage of criminal history information is seriously incomplete, but that is a problem already on its way to being solved. Meanwhile, there is utility in checks that use even incomplete computer records.

Third, local police departments need to do more to enforce existing laws banning the unlicensed possession of guns in public places. Most robberies and many other violent crimes involve carrying guns through public spaces, behavior that is already illegal (except for the tiny fraction of the population with a carry permit) nearly everywhere in the nation. There is, however, little enforcement of carry laws—the average police officer makes less than one carry arrest every two years.

New technologies may enable police officers to detect gun-sized metal objects at a distance, thereby improving their ability to identify likely carriers of concealed guns. Meanwhile, police departments could codify the knowledge of veteran officers and conduct research to develop new knowledge that would improve officers' ability to identify which individuals on the street are carrying concealed weapons. This research, and training based on it, could improve the average officer's "batting average" in stop-and-frisk street searches and thereby reduce complaints about arbitrary and unwarranted searches.

While increased carry arrests probably would not stop many offenders from carrying guns to commit specific planned crimes, it could reduce the casual daily carrying that is so common among serious criminals. This in turn could discourage the weakly motivated, unplanned crimes that occur as a byproduct of a criminal's daily life, such as a robber coming across a "good score" and impulsively pulling out his gun to commit an opportunistic robbery, or getting into an argument and committing an unpremeditated shooting.

None of these proposals are radical, politically impractical, or inordinately expensive. They are politically achievable because they place the burden of gun control largely on criminals rather than on noncriminal gun owners. Unfortunately, they are also not particularly "sexy" or useful for grabbing a headline or getting featured on the television news. At this late date, however, it may be time to seriously consider proposals that have a chance of actually reducing violence rather than merely gaining votes or media coverage for their sponsors.

Key Websites

THE NEW YORK TIMES ON THE WEB—ISSUES IN DEPTH: GUN CONTROL

Among the things you will find on this site are: a state-by-state summary of the laws governing firearm ownership; a forum on whether there is a way to make sure that gun laws already in existence are enforced; a special report on rampage killers with a profile of the 102 killers in 100 rampage attacks examined by the *New York Times* in a computer-assisted study looking back more than 50 years. There is also an overview of recent school shootings and related lesson plans for teachers.

http://www.nytimes.com/library/national/index-guns.html

GUNCITE—GUN CONTROL AND THE SECOND AMENDMENT ISSUES

This site has an extensive amount of information in opposition to gun control. It present an in-depth analysis of the Second Amendment, including quotes from the Constitution and the Founding Fathers. You will find information on how often guns are used in self-defense and to commit violence. It presents alternatives to gun control, and examples from international gun control laws.

http://www.guncite.com

THE SUPREME COURT'S THIRTY-FIVE OTHER GUN CASES:
WHAT THE SUPREME COURT HAS SAID ABOUT THE SECOND AMENDMENT

David B. Kopel, "The Supreme Court's Thirty-Five Other Gun Cases: What the Supreme Court Has Said about the Second Amendment": Among legal scholars, it is conventional wisdom that the Supreme Court has said almost nothing about the Second Amendment. This article suggests that the Court has not been so silent as the conventional wisdom suggests. These cases suggest that the justices of the Supreme Court do now and usually have regarded the Second Amendment "right of the people to keep and bear arms" as an individual right, rather than as a right of state governments.

http://i2i.org/SuptDocs/Crime/35.htm#_ftnref85

COMPREHENSIVE BIBLIOGRAPHY
OF THE SECOND AMENDMENT IN LAW REVIEWS

This site contains a list and links to dozens of articles about the Second Amendment or gun control that have been published in law reviews.

http://www.saf.org/AllLawReviews.html

FIREARM INJURY CENTER

The Firearm Injury Center is dedicated to the reduction of firearm injuries and deaths. The Center provides comprehensive, objective, accurate information and analysis of firearms and related morbidity and mortality. The Center collaborates with policymakers, community-based organizations and agencies, and with individuals at local, regional, and national levels to support effective prevention strategies.
http://www.mcw.edu/fic

JURIST—THE LEGAL EDUCATION NETWORK

This site is a resource for individuals on all sides in the ongoing controversy over the legal status of guns in the United States. It has links to material in the following categories: news releases, current cases, statistics and reports, government agencies, advocacy groups, gun manufacturers, and the media.
http://jurist.law.pitt.edu/gunlaw.htm

Should We Abolish the Juvenile Court System?

Fear of crime, especially random violence perpetrated by juveniles, has become a great concern. It has served as the motivation for countless numbers of people to change their lifestyles, take self-defense classes, install home security systems, and carry handguns for protection. Moreover, fear of crime has influenced politicians and laypersons to adopt the position that imposing stiff criminal penalties is an effective way for society to express outrage over the transgressions of "out of-control" youth.

Getting tough on juveniles is not a contemporary phenomenon. Juveniles have been punished as adults for centuries. Prior to the seventeenth century, for instance, children were seen as being different from adults only in their size. Youngsters were perceived as being miniature adults and, therefore, subject to the same punishments as offenders who were decades older. Childhood was considered to end at about age five.

It was not until the seventeenth century that European church and community leaders successfully advanced the notion that children were weak and innocent and in need of guidance, protection, and socialization by adults. Consequently, childhood was prolonged, education became a priority, and societal norms emerged specifying age-appropriate behavior. Youngsters were no longer viewed as miniature adults. For the first time in recorded history, they were a separate and distinct group.

By the early 1800s, the belief emerged that juvenile and adult offenders should be incarcerated separately. This led to the establishment of special correctional institutions for youthful offenders. It was, however, not until 1899 that the first juvenile court was established in the United States. This uniquely American institution was a continuation of the premise that youthful offenders should be treated differently than their adult counterparts. Instead of deciding guilt or innocence, the court would ascertain whether youths were in need of treatment. Under the driving philosophy of the new court, it would serve as the benevolent parent, wanting only that which is in the best interest of the children. Consequently, instead of harsh, punitive sanctions that sought to deter, the court would seek long-term behavioral change by providing the guidance youths so woefully lacked from their natural parents. Sentences were to be customized to meet the needs of each juvenile so as to optimize the rehabilitative effects of court intervention.

In recent years discontent with juvenile court has emerged as a consequence of at least two factors. First, the definitions of childhood and age-appropriate behavior are once again in a state of flux. These changes are an outgrowth of the fact that the youth of today seem to be more predisposed toward violence than they were in the past. National crime data sources seem to support this view. Violent juvenile crime has increased by nearly 70 percent since 1986. Moreover, the violence perpetrated by juveniles is portrayed by the mass media as being more heinous than at any other time in history. People are fearful of falling victim to a generation that seemingly holds beliefs and values that diverge drastically from those of the rest of society.

Second, the "get tough" approach to dealing with criminals as seen throughout the justice system is increasingly being applied to juvenile offenders as well. The public has lost confidence in rehabilitation programs for juveniles. Polls show that 49 percent of Americans believe these programs are not successful, and 52 percent believe the punishments juveniles receive should be the same as those given adults. A Gallup poll found that 72 percent of Americans advocate the death penalty for juveniles who commit murder, as opposed to 24 percent in 1957.

James Wootton and Robert O. Heck, in "How State and Local Officials Can Combat Violent Juvenile Crime," contend that the juvenile court system is failing because it doesn't target the most dangerous young offenders. They say that juvenile justice officials are not recognizing that some delinquent youth are such a threat to the community that they must be held accountable and incarcerated. Under the current system, the seriously violent juvenile can become invisible by being mixed in with the general population of nonviolent and nonhabitual juvenile offenders. Wootton and Heck feel that the official failure to discriminate between minor offenders and hard-core criminal youth undermines the effectiveness of the entire system.

David C. Anderson is not ready to give up on the juvenile court system. In "When Should Kids Go to Jail?" he points out that as long as rehabilitative programs do not expose the public to more crime than prison does, they are worth pursuing. They create positive experiences for youngsters coming out of chaotic social environments (at lower financial cost than prison), and they send a broad message about a society's willingness to help young people in trouble. Anderson believes rehabilitation holds enough promise to warrant continued experimentation with programs that might still produce real cuts in recidivism.

How State and Local Officials Can Combat Violent Juvenile Crime

James Wootton and Robert O. Heck

The New Face of Juvenile Crime

Growing numbers of young people, often from broken homes or so-called dysfunctional families, are committing murder, rape, robbery, kidnapping, and other violent acts.... [T]hese emotionally damaged young people, growing up without faith, fathers, or families, often are the products of sexual or physical abuse. They live in an aimless and violent present; have no sense of the past and no hope for the future; and act, often ruthlessly, to gratify whatever urges or desires drive them at the moment. They commit unspeakably brutal crimes against other people, and their lack of remorse is shocking.... They are the ultimate urban nightmare, and their numbers are growing. The number of juveniles arrested for violent crimes has increased nearly 60 percent over the last ten years:

- From 1985 to 1993, the number of murder cases involving 15-year-old juveniles increased 207 percent. Arrests of 18-year-old to 20-year-old males for murder over the same period increased 119 percent.

- From 1988 to 1992, the number of juveniles involved in aggravated assaults increased 80 percent to 77,900; the number involved in robberies went up 52 percent to 32,900; and the number involved in rapes rose 27 percent to 5,400. Overall, juvenile court cases increased 26 percent. If trends of the past ten years continue, arrests of juveniles for violent crimes will double by the year 2010.

- From 1989 to 1993, transfers of juveniles to adult court because of delinquency increased 41 percent to 11,800 cases; for crimes against persons, the number of transfers increased 115 percent to 5,000 cases.

From *The Heritage Foundation* (October 28, 1996). Copyright © 1996. Reprinted with the permission of The Heritage Foundation.

- Of 1,471,200 juvenile court cases in 1992, personal offenses were up 56 percent to 301,000; property offenses were up 56 percent to 842,000; and public order offenses were up 21 percent to 255,900.

Young Victims

Young people ages 12 to 17 are the most frequent victims of violent crime. They are raped, robbed, or assaulted at five times the rate of adults 35 years old or older.... Overall, the sad fact is that crime has seriously affected teenagers' lives, especially those who live in neighborhoods seriously hurt by crime, drugs, and gangs. The effects are insidious and long-standing. Teenagers protect themselves by carrying weapons, skipping school, changing their routes to and from classes, changing friends, or letting their grades slip. For many young Americans, the carefree days of adolescence are a nostalgic fantasy.

Even more shocking than the sheer volume of violent juvenile crime is the brutality of the crime committed for trivial motives: a pair of sneakers, a jacket, a real or imagined insult, a momentary cheap thrill. For example:

- A 59-year-old man out on a morning stroll in Lake Tahoe was fatally shot four times by teenagers "looking for someone to scare." The police say the four teenagers—just 15 and 16 years old—were "thrill shooting."
- A 12-year-old and two other youths were charged with kidnapping a 57-year-old man and taking a joy ride in his Toyota. As the man pleaded for his life, the juveniles shot him to death.
- A 14-year-old boy was murdered while trying to reclaim a $2,500 stereo system he had received from his grandfather. Five juveniles, ranging in age from 15 through 17 years, were charged with the crime.

Seasoned big-city homicide detectives have a hard time coming to grips with the horror of these kinds of cases: The crimes are senseless, the motives banal, and the perpetrators all so young. These shocking incidents—which occur in America's suburbs as well as its inner cities—are creating a growing consensus among the American people: They have had enough. Lenient sentencing based strictly on age is no longer acceptable for crimes of this magnitude.

Loss of Public Confidence

Polls show that Americans are unhappy with the system as it is: 49 percent believe rehabilitation programs for juveniles are not successful, 52 percent believe the punishments juveniles receive should be the same as those given adults, and 83 percent think juveniles who commit two or more crimes should receive the same sentencing as adults. A 1995 Gallup poll found that

72 percent of Americans also advocate the death penalty for juveniles who commit murder, as opposed to 24 percent in 1957.

Teenagers themselves take a hard stance on how their peers should be treated if they commit violent crimes. Over 93 percent believe that those accused of murder or rape should be tried as adults. Moreover, they do not believe these offenders should receive special consideration because of their age. This is consistent with broad public, judicial, and law enforcement sentiment, which generally has favored holding juveniles more accountable for their criminal actions in recent years.

The juvenile justice system that prevails in many states today does juvenile criminals no favors by being lenient....

Why Today's Juvenile Justice System Is Failing

Since 1899, when Illinois adopted the first Juvenile Court Act, America's juvenile courts have been unable to deal effectively with the violent juvenile criminal. Law enforcement officers and a growing number of private citizens realize that this continuing failure undermines the credibility of the whole juvenile justice system.

The ultimate price for this failure, of course, is paid by innocent citizens. For example, only hours after returning home from a special school program in Costa Rica, Cindy Del Carmen Villalba, an honor student at Rutgers University, was killed in a botched robbery attempt. Corie Miller, age 17, and two accomplices were charged in her death. Miller had been eluding police for about a week when the slaying occurred. He had fled a Paterson, New Jersey, "get-tough" rehabilitation program that was supposed to be a "last ditch effort to reform him." In the case of this habitual juvenile offender, it took the murder of a young, intelligent girl with a bright future to force the justice system to take a second look and finally adopt a tougher stance.

Failure to Target Serious Habitual Offenders

In many states, the greatest single weakness of the effort to combat juvenile crime is a simple failure to target the most dangerous young offenders. This weakness arises from a reluctance on the part of juvenile justice officials to admit that there is a point at which a delinquent youth becomes such a threat to the community that he or she must be held accountable and incarcerated. Under the current system, the seriously violent juvenile can become invisible by being mixed in with the general population of nonviolent and nonhabitual juvenile offenders. Overwhelmingly, most urban young people who get arrested for a crime get arrested only once; seldom are they a serious or long-term threat to the safety of other citizens. Put another way, not all juvenile delinquents are alike, and very few are serious habitual offenders. The official failure to discriminate between minor offenders and hard-core criminal youth undermines the effectiveness of the entire system.

The most active juvenile delinquents also are the most dangerous. Often invisible to the officials who preside over the system, they are painfully visible to the victims they assault, rob, and kill. Official failure to develop credible control measures to suppress habitual juvenile offenders also sows the seeds of racial prejudice. With the rise of juvenile crime, an increasingly angry and insecure public tends to look upon all juveniles, particularly black male teenagers, as threats to the community. Most juvenile offenders, however, are not: 58 percent of young black males never have any contact with the police; and of the other 42 percent, an overwhelming majority do not go on to become SHOs. It is therefore vital that state and local officials, as well as taxpayers, begin to think and act differently toward the occasional juvenile delinquent. The SHO, on the other hand, is a career criminal in the making.

The Information Gap

Chronic offenders usually can be identified solely on the basis of their juvenile records. This evidence, however, normally does not accumulate until after the youth's 16th birthday. If additional factors describing the youth's school performance and home situation are included, the age at which youthful chronic offenders can be identified and an intervention mounted may be moved up several years.

In reality, these young criminals are shunted in and out of state and local agencies by bureaucrats who are supposed to be running the system but who often seem to lack a collective awareness of the kind of young people they are processing. Too often, they are oblivious to the repeated and increasingly serious nature of the behavior of these young criminals. This official failure to share information can occur for many reasons: because it is not required by state law, because of bureaucratic inertia or lack of imagination, or even because of simple negligence. It is a key weakness in the current system. Most of the juvenile codes in the United States contain statutory language indicating that the juvenile judge should consider police reports; field interview reports; citations; social history information (such as data on school, family, and work); drug involvement information; motor vehicle operation information; associates' history; offense digests; victim accounts; and other relevant information, including medical and juvenile victimization data. Only rarely, however, is this information used or shared among youth service agencies; it often is not even made available to the presiding judge.

Declining Police Morale

The continuing failure of the juvenile justice system in many states contributes to defeatism and low morale among local police. Police officers frequently do not treat juvenile crime the same as they treat crime committed by adults. Since no one else in the criminal justice system seems to be serious about punishing juvenile criminals, police officers often feel they will be wasting their time if they pursue these cases with the same zeal they display in pursuing adult criminals. They have learned from painful and frustrating personal experience that spending street time trying to suppress juvenile crime by arrests is futile; nothing will be done to the young criminals, who will just be allowed back out on the streets. As a result, many patrol officers shift juvenile crime problems to the local department's juvenile unit, transferring both the problem and the responsibility to a specialized unit that already is overloaded.

How to Identify Serious Habitual Offenders

In every community, there is the potential for only 2 percent of the juvenile offender population to be responsible for up to 60 percent of the violent juvenile crime. These serious repeat offenders, who all too often eventually become adult career criminals, bleed the life from the community, endangering public safety and undermining economic stability.

In general, only 25 to 35 juveniles in every 100,000 members of the population will engage in criminal activity that matches the Serious Habitual Offender pattern.... [T]his means that 0.03 percent to 0.04 percent of all juveniles between 14 and 17 years old will be SHOs. At the same time, for each SHO, four other juveniles are at risk of becoming SHOs themselves.

Profile of a SHO

... The typical SHO is male, 15 years and 6 months old. He has been arrested 11 to 14 times, exclusive of status offenses, and 5 times for felonies. He comes from a dysfunctional family; and in 46 percent of cases, at least one of his parents also has an arrest history. He has received long-term and continuing social services from as many as six different community service agencies, including family, youth, mental health, social services, school, juvenile, or police authorities, and continues to drain these resources for years before he is finally incarcerated as a career criminal.

The typical SHO's family history follows a classic pattern of social pathologies: 53 percent of his siblings also have a history of arrest; and in 59 percent of these cases, there is no father figure in the home. The absence of a father is particularly destructive for boys; only 2 percent of SHOs are female. Furthermore, 68 percent of these offenders have committed crimes of violence, 15 percent have a history of committing sex crimes, and 51 percent have a reported missing or runaway record. If a broken family characterized by physical or sexual abuse is an early indicator of criminal behavior, then virtually all of these serious habitual offenders fit this category. Not surprisingly, these findings are consistent with the Heritage Foundation's widely reported analysis of the true root causes of violent crime, particularly the crimogenic conditions associated with broken or dysfunctional families.

In fact, SHOs do not consider the crimes they have committed to be all that bad. Forty-five percent are gang members, 64 percent associate with other serious habitual offenders, and 75 percent abuse drugs. School, social, and employment experiences are not good experiences for SHOs, who invariably have no moral compass. The SHO seems to feel that, no matter what he does, the system barely notices. The effect inevitably is to reinforce his criminal inclinations; when released from a state prison, for example, one in 30 of these offenders probably will commit murder.

Recent empirical evidence shows that illegal drug use among the young is on the rise. It is worth noting, therefore, that a significant majority of all SHOs use or sell illegal drugs and often become addicted themselves. Illegal drug use and alcohol abuse tend to be regular features of their criminal conduct. Drugs, in particular, are part of the criminal scene of these juvenile offenders, and the use and sale of drugs contributes significantly to a SHO's other criminal activity. The need to purchase illegal drugs, combined with the warped hedonism of the addict, shapes and drives much of the criminal activity of this class of criminals.

...

Cutting Short a Criminal Career

For law-abiding citizens, the career criminal is Public Enemy Number One. By using modern information technology and case management as embodied in Serious Habitual Offender Comprehensive Action Programs, law enforcement officers and local government officials can target and track society's most dangerous criminals. Almost without exception, the adult career criminal was a serious habitual offender as a juvenile. Once again, this is a very small minority of the population: 94 percent of the juveniles arrested for a criminal offense are never arrested again, 4 percent are arrested on a regular basis, and only 2 percent are arrested repeatedly and go on to become serious habitual offenders and career criminals. Career criminals exhibit common patterns of behavior, as well as a relationship between age and criminal behavior. Unfortunately, however, today's juvenile justice and adult criminal justice systems are not adequately linked.

Since both the volume and intensity of juvenile crime have increased and are likely to escalate in the future, it is no longer feasible to wait until these career criminals reach adulthood to protect society from their actions. There are stages in the life of the typical career criminal.

Stages of Development

In the first stage of criminal development, ... these serious habitual offenders come from abusive, broken, or neglectful homes.... [S]tate and local officials can design an early intervention strategy for juveniles who are at risk of becoming serious habitual offenders and career criminals. Such a strategy can focus community resources, including private-sector charitable, social, and religious institutions, on potential and active SHOs and stop their criminal careers before they gain momentum.

In the second stage of the criminal's development, from 13 to 18 years of age, ... judges and other state and local criminal justice officials answer a critical question: Is the offender, based on his record, likely to respond to intensive intervention by social service agencies, or is he in fact a youthful career criminal who cannot be rehabilitated and should be locked up? State corrections officials simply do not know how to rehabilitate some violent young criminals who pose such a clear danger to society that they must be separated from the community and controlled....

From the vantage point of public safety, the best that state and local officials can do with the incorrigible juvenile SHO when the crime is serious is to try him as an adult, sentence him as an adult, and require him to serve at least 85 percent of his sentence, as specified by the truth-in-sentencing laws called for in recent federal legislation and enacted in 22 states. This would mean that a 15-year-old serious habitual offender who is given 20 years for second-degree murder would serve at least 17 years before being released at age 32. Thus, the serious offender would have spent his highest crime years locked up, unable to prey on more victims.

During the third stage of a criminal's career, from 18 to 30 years of age, ... state and local criminal justice officials complete criminal histories of career offenders at the time they are arrested. The police, prosecutors, and judges know instantly that they are dealing with a SHO and not a petty or first-time offender. Currently, however, an adult criminal's previous juvenile records are not available to the system in most jurisdictions. As a result, 18-year-olds with lengthy records of serious and violent crime frequently are treated as first-time offenders.

A New Policy to Combat Violent Juvenile Crime

America's juvenile and criminal justice system still works too slowly to be effective in identifying and incarcerating career criminals. Congress can assist state and local officials with money, technology, and advice—and by removing federal mandates in the juvenile judicial system—but controlling and combating serious crime remains the responsibility primarily of state and local government. State and local leaders can take a variety of concrete steps to combat the scourge of violent crime, especially crimes committed by juveniles. Innovative police methods like those implemented in cities like Houston and New York are reducing the rate of violent crime.... [S]tate and local leaders can take three other steps to stop these criminal careers before they run their destructive course:

- *Target and track serious habitual offenders.* Enact legislation at the state level that enables local officials to share crucial juvenile case files and establish an effective Serious Habitual Offender Comprehensive Action Program in their local jurisdictions. SHOCAP can make available to police and state law enforcement officers, as well as judicial and corrections officials, the information they need to identify and respond to the most dangerous young criminals in their communities.

- *Try as adults all juveniles who commit heinous crimes.* Enact state laws to try juvenile offenders as adults for specific violent offenses. Under Title I of Representative McCollum's Violent Youth Predator Act of 1996, a juvenile criminal 14 or more years of age who is convicted of a serious federal violent crime or "a major drug trafficking offense" automatically can be tried as an adult. States should consider similar legislation for state offenses.

- *Enact truth-in-sentencing laws.* Pass legislation requiring all violent offenders, including juveniles tried as adults, to serve at least 85 percent of their sentences. Thus far, 22 states have adopted such laws. As the bipartisan Council on Crime in America has concluded, probation, parole, and other forms of nonincarceration often take the place of prison, even for violent offenders. More than half of convicted violent felons still are not sentenced to prison. This must end.

Conclusion

Congress can encourage state and local officials in their efforts to combat juvenile crime. The Violent and Repeat Juvenile Offender Act of 1996 sponsored by Senator Orrin Hatch and former Senate Majority Leader Robert Dole would allow states to try the most serious violent juvenile offenders (those charged with federal offenses) as adults. In many respects, this bill complements the Violent Youth Predator Act of 1996 sponsored by Representative McCollum. Both bills also give financial assistance to the states.

... The war to defeat the growing menace of violent juvenile crime must be fought and won by state and local officials who are smart, tough, and tenacious.... Today's serious habitual offenders are tomorrow's career criminals. Children who look more like victims of abuse and neglect than criminals at age 13 may well be engaged in repeatedly committing the community's most serious and violent offenses from ages 14 to 17. They are a serious and growing threat to public safety.

No

David C.
Anderson

When Should Kids Go to Jail?

While America's latest crime wave appears to be subsiding, the legitimate fears it aroused in urban America leave a powerful political legacy. Along with new police strategies and more prisons, legislators continue to call for harsher treatment of juvenile offenders long granted special status because of a historic belief in the diminished culpability of children and adolescents. Nearly all states now permit the "waiver" of youngsters charged with serious crimes to adult courts; in more than half, legislatures have specifically excluded those charged with certain crimes from juvenile court jurisdiction. In some cases the exclusions apply to children as young as 13. Legislation moving forward in the current Congress would expand adult federal court jurisdiction over offenders as young as 14 and give prosecutors, rather than judges, the power to transfer a juvenile case to adult court.

Therein lies an important debate. The nation [has witnessed] the one-hundredth anniversary of the first juvenile court, established in Chicago by Progressive Era reformers in 1899. It formally recognized that childhood should exist in the eyes of the criminal law. Youth, Progressives believed, can partly excuse even violent misbehavior and always permits hope for rehabilitation. Is that historic commitment really obsolete?

The question remains germane even as juvenile crime trend lines turn down, because demographics suggest a possible new crime wave. Scholars like James Alan Fox of Northeastern University have predicted a "baby-boomerang" 20 percent increase in the juvenile population and juvenile crime by 2005. The Justice Department predicts a doubling of juvenile arrests for violent crime by 2010.

From *The American Prospect* (May–June 1998). Copyright © 1999 by The American Prospect, Inc. Reprinted with the permission of The American Prospect, P.O. Box 772, Boston, MA 02102-0772. All rights reserved.

The Senate Judiciary Committee report on the new juvenile crime bill relies heavily on such predictions to justify treating more juvenile offenders as adults. Defenders of special treatment find themselves hampered by the history of the juvenile court, whose usefulness has fallen into real question as it has succumbed to an advanced identity crisis.

The Whole Child

The Illinois Juvenile Court Act of 1899, which established the Chicago court, was based on the British idea of *parens patriae*. It granted the state the power to intervene on behalf of children when their natural parents failed to provide care or supervision. "Jane Addams and the dauntless women of Hull House," who established the new court, "strove to develop a safe haven, a space to protect, to rehabilitate and to heal children, a site of nurturance and guidance, understanding and compassion."... Judges serving in the court were to receive social science and child development training so that they could craft sentences in the best interest of the "whole child."

The idea spread rapidly. Thirty-two states had set up juvenile courts or probation services by 1910; by 1925, they existed in all but two states. The belief that a court should take over the nurture and discipline of troubled youth informed both philosophy and procedures.... [T]he role of the juvenile court judge was to strengthen the child's belief in himself and make available to him all of the support and encouragement from outside the court that the judge could harness on his behalf."

...

In the 1960s, pressures from both the left and the right began to move treatment of juveniles away from the original vision. In the early juvenile courts, *parens patriae* meant substituting the benevolence of an individual judge for the adult court's adversarial process, fact-finding by juries of peers, guaranteed rights to counsel and cross-examination, and protection against self-incrimination. It also meant indeterminate sentences—locking up youngsters in treatment until the adults in charge agreed that they were rehabilitated, rather than for fixed periods of time. That was all well and good so long as juvenile court judges and treatment administrators were fair-minded, insightful, and caring. Where they weren't, juvenile offenders were routinely exposed to gross miscarriages of justice.

The Supreme Court recognized the problem in the 1967 case of 15-year-old Gerald Gault, who was charged with making an obscene phone call. A juvenile court judge ordered him to training school for six years; in adult court, the same case was worth a $50 fine or two months in jail.

In its ruling, the court rejected the whole idea of *parens patriae* and concluded that traditional juvenile justice violated the Fourteenth Amendment's guarantee of due process. "Juvenile court history has again demonstrated that unbridled discretion, however benevolently motivated, is frequently a poor substitute for principle and procedure," the court wrote.

The *Gault* decision upheld a juvenile defendant's right to protection against self-incrimination, to notice and counsel, and to question witnesses. The result was to bring lawyers into juvenile court for both the prosecution and defense and to force greater objectivity on the proceedings. While this curbed some of the abuse, it also curbed the capacity of judges to deal with the offender's broader problems.

...

Through the 1970s and early 1980s, responding to pressure from a crime-weary public, legislatures began pushing for punishment rather than treatment, especially of youngsters who looked like "hard-core" juvenile career criminals. They required juvenile courts to impose determinate or mandatory minimum sentences based on the severity of the crime rather than the needs of the offender. Some juvenile courts adopted the more punitive approach without any prodding from a legislature.

Juveniles sentenced to confinement, meanwhile, all too often wound up in training schools or detention centers that mocked the historic commitment to therapy, education, and rehabilitation. Inquiries and lawsuits during the 1970s and 1980s found juvenile inmates regularly subjected to systematic humiliation, solitary confinement in squalid cells, beatings, and homosexual assaults.

...

The rate of confinement for juveniles rose from 241 per 100,000 to 353 per 100,000 between 1975 and 1987, according to one national study. Another found that while the number of juveniles in the population declined by 11 percent between 1979 and 1989, the number locked up in institutions rose by 30 percent.

States also encouraged the shift of more juvenile cases to adult courts by either lowering the age of adult court jurisdiction for crimes or giving judges or prosecutors discretion to order waivers. The trend continued despite research demonstrating that such measures were having less than the desired effect. Adult courts are typically far more lenient with property offenders than are juvenile courts. And in states where judges supervised transfer of juvenile cases to adult courts, they tended to send up many more burglary and larceny cases than robberies, rapes, and murders. The property offenders therefore benefited from the "punishment gap," getting off with a year or two of lightly supervised probation, the routine in adult court, when the juvenile judge might have ordered them into a youth prison.

Add Crack Cocaine and Stir

The juvenile court's identity crisis was therefore well advanced by the mid-1980s, when crime rates spiked as crack dealers and gun dealers began aggressive distribution of their products to willing markets of young people. Juvenile delinquency cases not only increased; they involved more violence.

Howard Snyder, a researcher for the National Center for Juvenile Justice, found that delinquency caseloads rose 23 percent between 1989 and 1993, nearly three times the percentage increase in the juvenile population. Juvenile offenses against the person (homicide, rape, robbery, assault) rose 52 percent, compared with a 15 percent increase for drug and property crimes. Weapons-law cases increased by 87 percent.

The statistics underlay a lurid popular perception. The news and entertainment media discovered the drug issue in general and crack in particular during the late 1980s, giving broad play to the teenage drug dealer turned outlaw millionaire, an image of adolescent fantasy come horribly true. This only deepened questions about the credibility of juvenile courts. Young thugs were driving luxury cars, flaunting designer warm-ups and gold chains, arming themselves with assault weapons and paying their mothers' rent. Did they suffer from deprivation and a poor self-image? Were they really going to be helped by fatherly judges and caring social workers? Wouldn't they, not to mention the rest of us, be better served by a heavy dose of grown-up punishment?

The idea could drive even sober academics to feverish prose. James Q. Wilson, an influential political scientist at the University of California at Los Angeles, wrote of "innocent people being gunned down at random, without warning and almost without motive, by youngsters who afterwards show us the blank, unremorseful face of a seemingly feral, presocial being." William Bennett, with John DiIulio and John Walters, describes "'superpredators—radically impulsive, brutally remorseless youngsters … who murder, assault, rape, rob, burglarize, deal deadly drugs, join gun-toting gangs, and create serious communal disorders.... [N]ot even mothers or grandmothers are sacred to them."

While such rhetoric rings powerful chimes with the public, should it drive public policy? However legitimate, fear and loathing inspired by excesses of some juvenile criminals at the height of the crack plague can inhibit careful thinking about a problem whose practical and moral complexities demand more than a turn to harsher punishments.

The majority of young people who break the law are not feral, presocial predators. Though juvenile violence increased at a shocking rate during the late 1980s, the more than 2,000 homicides reported each year remain a tiny percentage of all juvenile crime. Of the 1.4 million arrests referred to juvenile courts in 1992, 57 percent involved property offenses as the most serious charge, while 21 percent involved crimes against the person. There is real danger that legislative nets cast to capture the "superpredators" will sweep in thousands of lesser fry as well, at appalling social and financial cost.

Furthermore, whatever goals the move against special treatment might accomplish, greater public safety does not appear to be one of them. A Florida study published in 1996 matched 2,738 juvenile delinquents transferred to adult courts with a control group that remained in the juvenile system. "By every measure of recidivism employed, reoffending was greater among transfers than among the matched controls," the researchers stated. A 1991 study compared juveniles tried in New York adult courts with New Jersey youngsters whose cases remained in juvenile court. It, too, found higher recidivism rates and prompter new arrests for the New York youngsters.

An ethically sensible and potentially effective policy on juvenile crime should include three elements: broader crime control, social work outside the criminal courts, and a reconception of juvenile justice.

Crime Control

By now the accumulating evidence documents overwhelmingly that the burst of youth crime in the late 1980s was caused by the rapid spread of drugs and guns. What to do about drugs remains uncertain. The crack epidemic appears to be expiring more as a result of natural causes than of smart policy, with saturated markets, aging addicts, and a skeptical new generation of street kids. But guns, in this context, are worth discussing.

Franklin Zimring of the Earl Warren Legal Institute, Alfred Blumstein of Carnegie Mellon University, and others have pointed out that guns account for the entire recent increase in youth homicide. In a striking article published in the *Valparaiso University Law Review* last spring, Zimring, a law professor at the University of California at Berkeley, noted that the number of reported killings committed with guns by youngsters between the ages of 10 and 17 increased sharply after 1984, from about 500 to more than 1,000. The number of nongun homicides remained stable through those years, at slightly fewer than 500.

"If there were a large group of 'new, more violent juvenile offenders,' that was the proximate cause of explosive increases in homicide," Zimring writes, "one would expect the increase in killing to be spread broadly across different weapon categories." Instead, it appears that "a change in hardware rather than a change in software was the principal cause of higher youth homicide." In that light, the most effective response looks like aggressive gun control focused on juveniles, backed up by the sort of innovative policing now credited with reducing juvenile gun use and homicides in Kansas City, Boston, and New York.

Social Work

Beyond programs designed to deal with youngsters after arrest, students of juvenile crime remain fascinated with the idea of intervening in the lives of children and teenagers "at risk" of delinquency in hopes of averting criminal behavior before it starts. Research documents some success. The most famous study was of the Perry Preschool, in Ypsilanti, Michigan, which provided two years of enriched schooling and weekly home visits to small children from poor minority families. By the time the kids had turned 27, half as many had been arrested as a control group that did not benefit from the enriched classes.

···

In 1996, a team of researchers from RAND led by Peter Greenwood reviewed seven such studies and calculated that day care/home-visit programs could reduce by 24 percent the number of crimes the client children could be expected to commit. The group also reviewed programs that give parents special training to deal with children who have begun to behave disruptively in school and at home; the training was found to reduce the youngsters' eventual juvenile criminality by 29 percent.

···

The RAND researchers attempted to estimate the cost-effectiveness of such approaches in comparison with increased incarceration resulting from California's new Three Strikes Law. They found that if fully applied across the state, two of the social work approaches, parent training and graduation incentives, were more cost-effective; taken together, they could reduce crime by 22 percent at a cost of about $900 million per year....

These results should be regarded with caution. The RAND study is a self-consciously artificial exercise designed to provoke pointed comparison rather than nail down a policy choice. It is based on necessarily speculative assumptions about how the effectiveness of well-resourced and well-managed pilot programs will "decay" as they are massively expanded. It also attempts to estimate the number of crimes children might commit over the course of their lives if they don't benefit from the programs, an imponderable calculation. Yet however speculative, the results remain tantalizing; they certainly warrant close attention to preventative social work as part of a juvenile crime strategy.

Juvenile Justice

... [S]cholars continue to believe in the need for a separate court that recognizes the possibility of rehabilitation for youthful offenders. They have been encouraged by recent research suggesting, contrary to decades of pessimistic findings, that rehabilitative programs can make a difference to the lives of delinquent youth.

They point to a 1990 meta-analysis that weighed 80 evaluations of rehabilitation programs, distinguishing between those that took care to match services with the needs and learning styles of the offenders and those that did not. The "appropriate" programs were found to reduce recidivism by as much as 50 percent.

···

Such studies provide practical hope to shore up the moral case: So long as rehabilitative programs do not expose the public to more crime than prison does, they are worth pursuing. They create positive experiences for youngsters coming out of chaotic social environments (at lower financial cost than prison), and they send a broad message about a society's willingness to help young people in trouble. It's a valid argument, and it looks all the better with reason to believe continued experimentation with such programs might still produce real cuts in recidivism.

Key Websites

JUVENILE JUSTICE CLEARINGHOUSE

The Juvenile Justice Clearinghouse is designed to be your one-stop website for juvenile justice information, programs for at-risk youth, and employment opportunities within this field.

http://www.fsu.edu/~crimdo/jjclearinghouse/jjclearinghouse.html

THE JUVENILE JUSTICE HOME PAGE

This site provides an excellent history of juvenile court, links to research reports, statistics, and articles on increases in juvenile crime and resources for parents, families, and juveniles themselves.

http://home.earthlink.net/~ehumes/homejuv.htm

OJJDP—OFFICE OF JUVENILE JUSTICE AND DELINQUENCY PREVENTION

The OJJDP website is designed to provide information and resources on general areas of interest about juvenile justice and delinquency, including conferences, funding opportunities, and new publications, and the comprehensive strategy as a framework for communities to combat youth crime. The site provides a visual depiction of how cases typically proceed through the juvenile justice system. It also supplies data sets for juvenile arrests, court processing, and supplemental homicide statistics as well as providing statistic-focused publications. The site contains links to agencies and organizations that provide data and statistics on juvenile justice.

http://ojjdp.ncjrs.org

JUVENILE FEMALE OFFENDERS: A STATUS OF THE STATES REPORT, OCTOBER 1998—THE OFFICE OF JUVENILE JUSTICE AND DELINQUENCY PREVENTION

The juvenile female offender of the 1990s is likely to have been sexually or physically abused, to come from a single-parent home, and to lack appropriate social and work-related skills. In recent years, she is more likely to be under age 15 and more likely to be a woman of color than in the past. However, some patterns of delinquent offending by young women have changed since the 1980s. While young women are still less likely than young men to become involved in delinquency, violent delinquency in particular, in recent years the involvement of young female offenders with the juvenile court for delinquent offenses has increased. This increase has important implications for many state service-delivery systems, which often underestimate their numbers and therefore are ill-prepared to deal effectively with

female delinquents. This report provides a profile of important new developments in the offending patterns of the juvenile female offender.
http://ojjdp.ncjrs.org/pubs/gender/index.html

THE AMERICAN BAR ASSOCIATION (ABA) JUVENILE JUSTICE CENTER

The ABA Juvenile Justice Center is dedicated to monitoring legislative, policy, and administrative changes emerging in juvenile justice systems across the nation. The Center responds to a vast assortment of juvenile justice issues, and provides leadership to judges, practitioners, bar associations, youth workers, correctional agency staff, policymakers, and the like. The Center's current activities emphasize the right to effective assistance of counsel and the representation of delinquent youth, issues surrounding juveniles tried as adults, and conditions of confinement.
http://www.abanet.org/crimjust/juvjus

THE JUVENILE DEATH PENALTY TODAY:
DEATH SENTENCES AND EXECUTIONS FOR JUVENILE CRIMES

Victor L. Streib, "The Juvenile Death Penalty Today: Death Sentences and Executions for Juvenile Crimes," January 1973–June 1999: This is the fifty-sixth issue of this report, which was first launched on June 15, 1984. The goal of these reports is to collect in one place the best available data and information on the death penalty for juvenile offenders. These reports sketch the characteristics of the juvenile offenders who have been sentenced to death, who have been executed, and/or who are currently under death sentences, and of their crimes. Nonetheless, these reports almost invariably underreport the number of death-sentenced juvenile offenders due to difficulty in obtaining accurate data.
http://www.law.onu.edu/faculty/streib/juvdeath.htm

THE CRIMINAL JUSTICE CENTER

The Criminal Justice Statistics Center at Minnesota Planning is one of 52 Statistical Analysis Centers across the United States, District of Columbia, Puerto Rico, and Mariana Islands funded by the Federal Bureau of Justice Statistics. The center's mission is to collect and analyze data relating to crime and the justice system, provide accurate information and analysis on emerging and critical issues, and support informed policy decisions through long-range planning. The website also includes information on teen courts. Youth who commit minor offenses are experiencing consequences of their behavior not from the juvenile court system or a school disciplinary board but from a "jury" of their peers in teen court. In most situations, successful completion of the

program means that the youth will not have a juvenile record or, in the case of a school referral, will not be suspended or expelled.
http://www.mnplan.state.mn.us/cj

NATIONAL CRIMINAL JUSTICE REFERENCE SERVICE (NCJRS)

The National Criminal Justice Reference Service (NCJRS) is one of the most extensive sources of information on criminal and juvenile justice in the world. NCJRS responds to queries from law enforcement and corrections officials, lawmakers, judges and court personnel, and researchers. The NCJRS staff receives more than 5,000 requests each month from around the world.
http://www.ncjrs.org/ncjhome.htm

Have Mandatory Sentencing Laws Helped Stop Crime?

In the past thirty years there have been enormous changes in the philoso-phy and practice of sentencing and corrections. The strong emphasis on rehabilitation that had existed for the first seven decades of the twentieth century gave way to a focus on fairness and justice where sentences would reflect appropriate punishment for a crime.

In the 1980s and 1990s, law and order advocates attacked rehabilitation as coddling criminals. They wanted to implement policies that would limit the ability of judges and correctional officials to mitigate the harshness of crimi-nal sanctions. They advocated "get tough" proposals for mandatory mini-mum sentences and lengthy determinate sentences as methods for reducing criminal activities through incapacitation and deterrence.

Eventually every state in the nation adopted some type of mandatory minimum sentencing law. Most of these laws applied to crimes involving se-rious violence, drugs, or firearms. Another type of mandatory sentencing was tied to an individual's criminal record. These "habitual offenders" laws had long been used to require heavier-than-normal sentences for criminals con-sidered habitual or career because of the number and severity of their prior convictions.

Mandatory minimum statutes eliminate discretion to choose a sentence below, but not above, the state minimum. Under this sentencing method, a specific crime would carry a clearly identified sentence length, not a broad minimum and maximum. Parole release would be eliminated. Sentence lengths would be determined by guidelines that considered only the past his-tory of criminal activity and the current crime of conviction. For instance, a law might require a mandatory minimum sentence of ten years for a specif-ic drug offense. Upon conviction, the judge must impose a prison term of not less than ten years but may impose a longer term. The penalty cannot be reduced even if, in the opinion of the judge, the individual case warrants it.

As a result of mandatory sentencing laws, those sentenced to prison are spending more time in prison. Time served in prison has been the major factor contributing to the growth in inmates in state prisons.

Mandatory minimum laws also disproportionately affect minority offenders. African Americans constitute a large percentage of the people arrested for violent crimes and, thus, they are disproportionately affected by these changes in laws.

Joseph M. Bessette, in "In Pursuit of Criminal Justice," claims that mandatory sentencing laws have produced welcome changes. He notes that the public recommends prison sentences for a variety of violent and other serious crimes that are approximately three times longer than offenders actually serve. He says that by bringing punishment more in line with public judgments about what offenders deserve, we will incapacitate recidivists, more effectively deter would-be criminals, and enhance public confidence in our governing institutions. Finally, by reaffirming and enforcing the precepts of the moral order, we can provide essential institutional support for the good efforts of parents, preachers, and teachers to fashion a law-abiding community.

David B. Kopel, in "Sentencing Policies Endanger Public Safety," points out that mandatory sentencing laws and other tactics that drastically increase punishment for nonviolent drug offenders may *appear* to cause no problem for people who do not use narcotics, but, in truth, these laws and tactics threaten the safety of every American. Taxes and debt rose in the past decade, in part to help pay for more than doubling national prison capacity, and most of the prison space went to incarcerate people for nonviolent offenses. Today, prisons are bursting at the seams, and there is insufficient room for hard-core violent criminals because the space is already taken by nonviolent criminals serving mandatory minimum sentences. Kopel explains that mandatory minimums are the best thing that ever happened to violent criminals because they prevent judges from doing what they want, which is to put violent thugs away for a long time, and they force the prison system to waste precious space on nonviolent offenders. The violent criminals out on parole are given their opportunity to commit more crimes by a criminal justice system fixated on drugs.

Yes

In Pursuit of Criminal Justice

Joseph M.
Bessette

Despite evidence suggesting that much of American public policy closely, perhaps too closely, mirrors public desires (for example, Social Security, Medicare, and the federal college-loan program), this is hardly the case in how we punish violent criminals. Policymakers and criminal justice practitioners set punishment levels well below what the public considers appropriate. Indeed, our punishment practices reflect a pronounced disconnect between reasonable public opinion, on the one hand, and actual government policy, on the other.

Most Americans are skeptical of their criminal justice system, and properly so. Perhaps the single best measure of their dissatisfaction is the answer they give to a question regularly asked by the Gallup organization about the performance of the courts. In 1994, 85 percent of Americans maintained that the courts in their area dealt "not harshly enough" with criminals. There was almost no change in this level of dissatisfaction across a range of socio-demographic variables such as sex, race, age, education, income, and region. Although this question asks specifically about courts, it is likely that respondents treat courts as a surrogate for the entire criminal justice system, not distinguishing, for example, between courts and overly generous parole boards.

There is an empirical basis for the public's suspicion of insufficient harshness. According to the National Punishment Survey conducted by the Population and Society Research Center at Bowling Green State University in 1987, the public recommends prison sentences for a variety of violent and other serious crimes approximately three times longer than offenders actually serve. And, according to U.S. Department of Justice data on actual time

From *The Public Interest* (October 15, 1997). Copyright © 1997 by National Affairs, Inc. Reprinted with the permission of *The Public Interest*. All rights reserved.

served by those leaving state prisons, half the murderers serve seven years or less, half the rapists serve less than four years, half the robbers serve two years and three months or less, half of those convicted of felony assault (often called aggravated assault) serve one year and four months or less, and half the drug traffickers serve one year and two months or less. Altogether, half of the 54,000 violent offenders who were released from prisons in 36 states in 1992 served two years or less behind bars. These data include many offenders with prior records and many convicted of multiple offenses at one time.

Even these figures fail to capture the full picture, for large numbers of those convicted of felonies receive sentences of straight probation (a period of supervision in the community) rather than incarceration. In 1994, state courts throughout the nation sentenced 29 percent of convicted felons to probation with no incarceration, a total of 253,000 offenders, including 2,400 rapists, 5,500 robbers, over 16,000 persons convicted of aggravated assault, and 48,000 drug traffickers. It is hardly conceivable that the American people agree with the granting of straight probation to so many convicted felons and violent offenders.

...

Discretion Too Far

Another reason why punishments often fall short of public expectations is judicial leniency. Well-publicized reductions in judicial discretion in recent decades, brought about by sentencing guidelines and mandatory minimum-sentencing laws in the federal system and some states, have done little to change this. In the majority of criminal convictions throughout the country, judges retain extraordinary power to choose probation or prison, to determine the length of prison sentences, to throw out collateral convictions, and to impose concurrent or consecutive sentences for the offenders with multiple convictions. Sometimes that discretion is exercised in ways that completely defy reasonable public judgments about just policy.

...

Finally, plea bargaining is often identified as a major cause of light sentences. Given the huge increase in judicial resources that would be necessary to give trials to all indicted felons, prosecutors and judges, it is said, are under enormous pressure to reach an accommodation with the accused: that is, to give them a break on the punishment in exchange for a plea of guilty. And, in fact, according to the Bureau of Justice Statistics, the vast majority of felony convictions in this country are the result of a guilty plea (89 percent) rather than a trial before a judge (5 percent) or jury (6 percent). As expected, those who plead guilty are, crime for crime, less likely to be sentenced to prison than those found guilty after trial. Moreover, if incarcerated, they receive shorter sentences.

Not every plea bargain, however, leads to overly lenient punishment.

Indeed, the term itself is deceptive because it implies that all pleas are the result of a bargain. That nine out of ten felony convictions result from the defendant's voluntary admission of guilt does not itself prove that in all or most of these cases the prosecutor offered a sentence reduction. Defendants, after all, have a right to plead guilty. That those who go to trial get stiffer sentences may reflect the fact that those charged with the most serious robberies, rapes, or assaults have a greater incentive to go to trial and hope for an acquittal. Moreover, in those cases where evidence problems render a conviction problematic, a prosecutor convinced of the defendant's guilt may decide that a few years in prison, or even felony probation, is better than taking the chance that the defendant will "walk." Thus, in some cases, plea bargains may result in more punishment than would a trial.

The Invisible Hand of Leniency

Some argue that the public, despite its dissatisfaction with current punishment levels, is unwilling to pay the costs of increased punishment. Yet this hardly seems tenable. Only 1.1 percent of all government spending in this country is devoted to building and operating all of our prisons and to running all of our probation and parole programs. Even doubling or tripling this amount would not raise corrections spending to more than a tiny fraction of all government spending. It is true, of course, that corrections costs are a higher fraction of state-government spending, since state governments finance most of the nation's prisons. But even here the proportion is in the range of 4 percent to 5 percent, far less than what is spent on education and social welfare. With the average American contributing about 30 cents per day to cover the nation's entire correctional budget (including probation and parole), insufficient resources can hardly explain why half the rapists are serving less than four years or why 253,000 convicted felons each year receive a straight probation sentence.

What, then, accounts for the divergence between public opinion and public policy? In important respects, punishment policy in the United States is the accumulation of millions of individual decisions each year: decisions about whether to arrest an individual; whether to prosecute him; whether to drop some charges or offer a break on the sentence through a plea bargain; whether to send the convicted offender to probation or prison; whether to imprison those who violate probation; how long to make prison sentences; whether to make sentences for multiple crimes concurrent or consecutive; whether to rescind good-time credits for misbehavior in prison; whether to parole from prison eligible offenders; and whether to return to prison those who violate the conditions of release. While we have excellent statistical information on the aggregate results of these decisions, the public is still essentially ignorant, in all but a few high-publicity cases each year, of the specific punishment decisions made in their community.

···

It follows that, in the vast majority of criminal cases, those who make the actual punishment decisions are free to do as they will within the usually broad confines of applicable state law. This allows two factors to come into play that help to weaken punishment. One is organizational overload. The thousands of criminal cases each year that are processed by county courts tax the resources of prosecutors, public defenders, judges, and local jail officials.

···

Similarly, prison officials are faced with the daunting task of managing growing prison populations in facilities that were typically designed to house many fewer inmates. It is not surprising that those who run prisons often support generous good-time policies, early-release mechanisms, or accelerated paroles in order to move bodies through the institution.

···

During the 1950s and 1960s, states made rehabilitation rather than punishment the central principle of penal policy. Probation became more widely used, along with indeterminate sentences, and liberal release practices. Parole boards began assessing the prisoner's fitness for release, not whether he had suffered a punishment commensurate with his crime. The predominance of this ideology of rehabilitation explains why the nation's prison population did not increase between 1960 and 1975 (and actually declined between 1960 and 1968) at the very time when serious crimes reported to the police more than tripled (from 3.4 million to 11.3 million), when the violent crimes of murder, rape, robbery, and aggravated assault increased three and one-half times (from 288,000 to one million), and when arrests for serious crimes increased two and one-half times.

Despite the fact that the rehabilitation approach has fallen out of public favor and one now rarely hears it publicly defended as the basis for sentencing adult offenders, approximately three-fourths of the states still retain the essential mechanisms of the rehabilitation ideology: the indeterminate sentence and discretionary parole-board release.

The Good Sense of the People

The National Punishment Survey revealed that the public is more discerning and reasonable than the critics of tougher punishment who so often decry the public's supposed mindless thirst for vengeance are willing to concede. For example, the public's recommendations were highly sensitive to the relative seriousness of the crime. The average recommended time in prison was 15 to 17 years for rape; 3 to 10 years for robbery, depending on the presence of a weapon and whether the victim was injured; 6 to 8 years for assault, depending on the extent of injury; and 2 to 5 years for burglary, depending on the amount stolen and whether the target was a commercial building or a home. Within the same crime categories, greater victim injury and increased property loss always resulted in higher recommended punishment.

Consider the four robbery scenarios outlined in the survey. In the first, the offender did not have a weapon but threatened to harm the victim unless the victim gave him money; the victim gave $10 and was not harmed. For this offense, 72 percent of the respondents recommended prison as the most severe sanction with an average term of 3 years and 10 months. In the second scenario, the facts were the same but for the addition of a weapon. For this robbery, 75 percent of the respondents recommended prison with an average term of 5 years and 8 months. In the third scenario, the offender robbed the victim at gun point of $1,000 and wounded him seriously enough to require hospitalization. Here 92 percent of the respondents recommended prison with an average term of 10 years and 3 months. In the fourth scenario, the offender shot the victim to death when the victim struggled during the robbery attempt. For this robbery and homicide, 30 percent of the respondents recommended the death penalty and another 67 percent recommended prison as the most serious penalty with an average term of 26 years.

Not only were the results of the survey highly responsive to variations in crime seriousness, there was no evidence here that Americans want to lock them up and throw away the key for any but the most violent criminals. In a word, the results of the survey seem eminently reasonable, however much tougher the American people are than the criminal justice system that operates in their name.

In its critique of the findings of the National Punishment survey, the National Council on Crime and Delinquency, one of the nation's leading anti-punishment groups, likened asking Americans what punishments they would mete out to criminals to questions such as "How many nuclear warheads does the United States need to defend against attack?" or "What proportion of deposits should banks hold in reserve to protect their customers?" Asking people who are generally uninformed very specific policy questions may reveal their state of ignorance, but their responses could hardly be taken seriously as the basis for policymaking.

Thus it does not matter how much punishment the American people think is appropriate for murderers, rapists, robbers, and burglars because, apparently, punishing criminals is a technical matter like designing strategic defense systems or fashioning the details of banking policy. Policymakers, it follows, are free to ignore the desires of an "uninformed" public.

Yet deciding how much punishment an offender deserves involves a moral judgment, not a technical one. To say that the moral judgments of the American people should not "be taken seriously as the basis for policymaking" is to reject no less than democracy itself.

Justice for All

Although complete freedom from crime is an unrealistic goal, a substantial reduction in serious and violent crime is not. The most constructive way to move toward that reduction, building upon recent encouraging trends, is to embrace standards of just punishment that approximate reasonable public judgments. Here the challenge lies primarily with state legislatures, for they are the original source of our punishment policies and practices. If the state penal codes themselves prescribe punishments well below public standards, then they should be rewritten and brought into line with public opinion. If judges are too lenient in how they exercise their sentencing discretion, then the legislature can establish presumptive sentences or mandatory minimums for serious offenders or recidivists. If parole boards are too generous in granting releases from prison, then parole can be restricted or even abolished (as about one-fourth of the states have done during the past two decades). And if insufficient judicial resources are resulting in large punishment discounts through plea bargaining, then the legislature should authorize and fund more judges, prosecutors, and public defenders.

By bringing punishment more in line with public judgments about what offenders deserve, we will incapacitate recidivists, more effectively deter would-be criminals, and enhance public confidence in our governing institutions. Finally, by reaffirming and enforcing the precepts of the moral order, we can provide essential institutional support for the good efforts of parents, preachers, and teachers to fashion a law-abiding community.

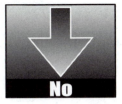

Sentencing Policies
Endanger Public Safety

David B.
Kopel

Since the 1980s, the United States has been engaged in the largest imprisonment program ever attempted by a democratic society. The number of persons incarcerated has soared to levels unknown in American history. In addition to the nearly 1,000,000 individuals in state and federal prisons and the more than 400,000 in city and county jails, there are over 2,000,000 persons on probation and more than 500,000 on parole.

...

The drastic growth of the combined state and federal prison population mainly is the result not of demographics, but of policy changes. Population growth accounted for almost 8 percent of the increase in prison inmates; increased crime, about 19 percent; and more arrests, slightly more than 5 percent. The great bulk of the surge, around 61 percent, was the result of decisions to send to prison offenders who otherwise would have been given an alternative sentence. An additional 7 percent resulted from an increase in time served.

There are no signs of the surge's abating.... At the rate prisoners are being added to the state and federal systems, the United States needs more than 1,100 new prison beds each week.

The average American prison system now operates at about 15 percent over capacity.... The Federal prison system is almost 40 percent over capacity.

Prison violence also has increased. Inmate assaults on guards have risen tenfold in the 1990s. Overcrowding also contributes to attacks on other prisoners, as two persons with histories of violent assault often are placed in a cell designed for one.

From *USA Today Magazine* (November 1, 1995). Copyright © 1995. Reprinted with the permission of The Society for the Advancement of Education.

The number of state and federal prisoners per 100,000 population tripled in the last two decades, and the United States now leads the world in the percentage of its population it keeps behind bars, with an incarceration rate of around 350 adults per 100,000 population. In contrast, the Australian imprisonment rate is about 90.

Paralleling the explosion of the numbers in prisons has been a surge in the jail population. (Prisons are state or federal facilities that hold convicted criminals. Jails are city and county facilities that hold persons sentenced to shorter terms, typically under a year. Persons arrested and not released on bail pending trial also are held in jail. Thus, at any given time, about half of a jail's population will be people who have not been convicted of a crime.) The number of jail inmates per capita in the United States has more than doubled since 1978 and now exceeds the total incarceration rate (jail plus prison) of most other democracies.

Total operating costs of state and federal prisons are approximately $13,000,000,000 a year. Adding in prison construction and the costs of city and county jails, the national incarceration budget is about $25,000,000,000.

···

Expensive as prisons can be, the incarceration of violent criminals is a tremendous bargain. At large, they can cause hundreds of thousands of dollars in damage each year. When harder-to-measure costs, such as the pain and suffering of victims, are considered along with the more quantifiable expenses (medical care of victims, funerals, and property destruction), it becomes clear that keeping a violent criminal in prison is an extremely efficient use of tax dollars.

However, state and federal prison systems are less and less likely to house repeat violent offenders. It is far from clear that incarcerating record numbers of individuals such as prostitutes and drug suppliers whose only offense is to facilitate a voluntary transaction between adults is a worthwhile expenditure of limited tax dollars.

More important than fiscal efficiency is the fundamental issue of public safety. As the state and federal governments have taken record numbers of prisoners in the war on drugs, violent criminals have found to their pleasant surprise that there is less and less room for them in prison.

Impact of the War on Drugs

As legislative bodies in the 1980s grew increasingly determined to prove that they were "doing something" in the war on drugs, mandatory minimum sentences for narcotics offenses became common. The expectation was that mandatory minimums would reduce the availability of drugs by curbing the number of suppliers. Instead, the result has been a living nightmare of barbaric punishment for small-time offenders, to the detriment of public safety.

In 1984, Congress began adding vast new numbers of mandatory minimums, particularly for crimes involving drug or firearms offenses. Since then, more than 60,000 individuals have been sentenced under these guidelines. Ninety-four percent of federal mandatory minimum cases involve four laws covering drugs or weapons. Beginning with New York's "Rockefeller Law" in 1973, almost every state has enacted its own mandatory minimums.

These mandatory minimums are extremely tough on narcotics offenses and make drug weight almost the sole factor in setting a sentence. For instance, possessing more than five grams of crack cocaine requires five years in federal prison. (An individual packet of sugar in a restaurant weighs about one gram.) The only factors other than drug weight that may be considered in the sentencing are if the defendant has prior convictions, in which case the mandatory minimum is raised, and if the U.S. attorney makes a motion stating that the defendant has provided "substantial assistance" in obtaining the conviction of another drug criminal, in which case the court has discretion to sentence the defendant to less than the mandatory minimum.

The federal mandatory minimums are not limited to persons who possess the particular quantities for sale. In 1988, Congress added conspiracy to commit a drug offense to the list of crimes with mandatory minimums. Thus, if a woman tells an undercover federal agent where to buy some LSD and the purchase is made from a person who possessed five grams of it, the woman, as a "conspirator," is subject to the same mandatory minimum as is the person who actually possessed the LSD. As a result of the sentencing guidelines and the mandatory minimums, one-quarter of all federal inmates are serving sentences of 15 years or more; half are serving sentences of over 7 years.

...

The Uniform Controlled Substances Act (UCSA) is a "model" state law being pushed in state legislatures nationwide. The act includes numerous instances requiring mandatory prison sentences. One factor is sale of drugs to a minor. Does a school janitor who pushes drugs to elementary school children deserve a severe, lengthy sentence? Does an 18-year-old high school student who asks his 17-year-old girlfriend to store a gram of cocaine in her jacket pocket temporarily until his older brother can buy it deserve an equally severe, lengthy sentence? Under the UCSA, the same mandatory sentence applies to both persons since they involved a minor in their drug crime. Similarly, does a California college student who brings four grams of psilocybin mushrooms home to Idaho for personal use on Christmas vacation deserve the same type of severe sentence meted out to someone who smuggles three pounds of heroin into the state? "Yes," is the answer, according to the UCSA, since both imported drugs into the state.

Mandatory minimums have the stated goal of ensuring that similar offenders receive similar sentences, but, in practice, perverse, unequal consequences often result. Mandatory minimums tend to fall hardest on people who are not habitual criminals (who already are covered by repeat offender laws). For instance, in 1989, Delaware enacted a three-year mandatory minimum, with no parole, for possession of 5 to 15 grams of an illegal substance. Seventy-two percent of the persons convicted under the new law had never before been imprisoned for any crime.

Drug dealers often recruit individuals known as "mules" for a single smuggling trip. When the mandatory minimums are applied to those low-level couriers, American taxpayers end up spending large amounts of money to imprison foreigners for years on end. A Sentencing Commission study of 1,100 cases found that one-fourth of all persons sentenced under the mandatory minimums were not American citizens. As more and more persons reject the idea of paying welfare to illegal aliens, it may be asked whether it is appropriate to spend so many tax dollars paying room and board for aliens within America's ultimate welfare state, the prison system.

Chief Justice William H. Rehnquist, not known for his lenient approach to crime, observed: "These mandatory minimum sentences are perhaps a good example of the law of unintended consequences. There is a respectable body of opinion which believes that these mandatory minimums impose unduly harsh punishment for first-time offenders—particularly for 'mules' who played only a minor role in a drug distribution scheme. Be that as it may, the mandatory minimums have also led to an inordinate increase in the federal prison population and will require huge expenditures to build new prison space...."

...

The Devastating Impact on Public Safety

Multiplying the risk of apprehension by the average sentence served upon conviction, Texas A&M University economist Morgan Reynolds found that the average 1990 murderer could expect to serve 1.8 years in prison. The expected punishment for murder fell by 20 percent from 1988 to 1990; for rape, 25 percent; and for robbery, 50 percent. From 1950 to 1990, the expected punishment for all serious crimes, taken as a whole, dropped by 65 percent. Simply put, crime pays.

In 1993, Sen. Phil Gramm (R.-Tex.) used the Reynolds expected-punishment calculations as proof of the need for mandatory minimums: "Mandatory minimum sentences deal with this problem directly. When a potential criminal knows that if he is convicted he is certain to be sentenced, and his sentence is certain to be stiff, his cost-benefit analysis changes dramatically and his willingness to engage in criminal activity takes a nosedive."

Yet, more than a decade after Congress imposed severe mandatory minimums for drug sales, it is apparent that criminal willingness to engage in illegal narcotics transactions has not taken "a nosedive." To the contrary, cocaine is cheaper, purer, and more readily available than it has been in decades.

...

Sociologist Robert Figlio points out that most violent crimes are perpetrated by a fairly small number of sociopaths. They start committing violent crimes early in life and continue doing so long after age 30, the age by which most other criminals have settled down. Figlio suggests that failing to incarcerate those repeat, violent offenders for lengthy periods greatly endangers public safety, and the reason those offenders are not incarcerated is that so much prison space is consumed by drug offenders.

Though inner-city delinquent teenagers may not have calculated the mathematical risks of arrest, they are well aware of how minimal punishments are for even the most serious armed, violent offenses. They can not help but infer that society really doesn't take violent crime seriously. Are they not right in their perceptions of today's criminal justice system, where first-offense burglary practically has been decriminalized? If a society is so intent on sending first-time drug vendors to prison leaving first-time muggers to go free, should it be surprising that burglary and mugging increase?

What kind of society treats mere possession of a drug more severely than drunk driving, even though drunk driving is, by definition, always dangerous to other persons and is known to cause the deaths of thousands of sober people every year? In contrast, possession of drugs generally is not dangerous to anyone except the possessor.

There is one other way in which mandatory minimums may encourage violent crime. It is possible that the prospect of mandatory minimums may increase the willingness of some offenders to commit murders in order to avoid detection. If the mandatory minimum sentence for a drug or gun possession crime is not much less than for homicide, some criminals will find murder a risk-aversive choice.

...

Whatever benefits the war on drugs has brought America, there has been a terrible price exacted by the violent criminals set free to make room for such offenders.... The fundamental flaw of the entire strategy of trying to control drug use through imprisonment is that it can not work, as free-market analysis demonstrates. In contrast, incarcerating violent criminals does work, and the removal of them from prison cells to make room for drug criminals replaces a policy that works with one that does not.

As long as a violent criminal is locked up, he will not endanger anyone except other prisoners and the prison guards. Imprison one armed robber, and there is one fewer armed robber on the street. Imprison half the armed robbers, and the armed robbery rate will decline about 50 percent. The same analysis applies to child abusers, burglars, and most other felons who repeatedly attack innocent people. The more of them are imprisoned, the less crime will occur while they are incarcerated.

In contrast, the imprisonment of one drug dealer (or the destruction of one drug distribution network) does not diminish the availability of narcotics for long. Nearly as soon as one dealer is removed, another will move in to take his place. The law of supply and demand states that as long as there is a demand for a product, a market will make it available at some price. Thus, removing one cocaine-addicted junkie who sells drugs on a street corner offers another the opportunity to do so. Likewise, removing one network of drug suppliers simply opens up a market for others. Allocating vast amounts of prison space to such easily replaced offenders is a dangerous waste of public resources.

Alternatives to Incarceration

As prison crowding increases, alternatives to incarceration are becoming more popular. Among these are electronic home detention, intensive supervised probation, and boot camps. Although all have merit in certain cases, thus far they have not reduced prison crowding significantly.

Instead, the large majority of convicts diverted into alternative programs tend to be individuals who would not have been imprisoned in the first place. Thus, a person who might have been sentenced to loosely supervised probation would be sentenced instead to home detention with electronic monitoring. For such programs to have any effect in reducing the prison capacity crisis (thereby enabling prisons to hold repeat violent offenders for longer periods), they must be used as alternatives to imprisonment, rather than to standard probation. One important step toward better use of alternatives would be to establish the presumption that they, rather than imprisonment, should be used in the large majority of first-time drug offenses.

Mandatory minimums and other tactics that drastically increase punishment for nonviolent drug offenders may appear to cause no problem for people who do not use narcotics. In truth, though, they threaten the safety of every American. While taxes and debt rose in the last decade, in part to help pay for more than doubling national prison capacity, most of the space went to incarcerate people for nonviolent offenses. Today, prisons are bursting at the seams, and there is insufficient room for hard-core violent criminals because the space already is taken by nonviolent criminals serving mandatory minimum sentences. Mandatory minimums are the best thing that ever happened to violent criminals, because they prevent judges from doing what they want, putting violent thugs away for a long time, and force the prison system to waste precious space on nonviolent offenders. The violent criminals out on parole are given their opportunity to commit more crimes by a criminal justice system fixated on drugs.

...

It is time for the fiasco to end. Prisons' primary mission is not the punishment of voluntary capitalist acts between consenting adults, even if they involve substances disapproved of by the majority. It is time for America's prisons to be devoted, as they were in previous, safer generations, to the incapacitation of violent criminals.

KEY WEBSITES

U.S. SENTENCING COMMISSION—JUST PUNISHMENT: PUBLIC PERCEPTIONS AND THE FEDERAL SENTENCING GUIDELINES

The Sentencing Reform Act of 1984 charged the U.S. Sentencing Commission with developing the "means of measuring the degree to which the sentencing, penal, and correctional practices are effective in meeting the purposes of sentencing...." To address these directives, the commission undertook a national survey to assess public opinion about just punishment for federal offenses.
http://www.ussc.gov/justpun.pdf

U.S. SENTENCING COMMISSION—SPECIAL REPORT TO THE CONGRESS: COCAINE AND FEDERAL SENTENCING POLICY, APRIL 29, 1997

This report contains the commission's recommendations on federal sentencing policy for cocaine offenses. The commission reached the unanimous conclusion that the penalty for simple possession of crack cocaine should be the same as for the simple possession of powder cocaine.
http://www.ussc.gov/newcrack.pdf

THE NOVEMBER COALITION FOUNDATION

The November Coalition Foundation is an organization of citizens whose lives have been affected by the U.S. government's present drug policy. The coalition is dedicated to educating the public about the destructive effects of the increase in the U.S. prison population due to the war on drugs. Their goal is to encourage those who have become outspoken critics of current policy.
http://www.november.org

BACKFIRE: WHEN INCARCERATION INCREASES CRIME

Todd R. Clear, "Backfire: When Incarceration Increases Crime": This paper examines various ways in which prisons may have inadvertently affected crime rates. The author notes that even though levels of imprisonment increased fivefold since 1973, crime rates have not dropped proportionately during this period. He argues that the crime-reducing aspects of imprisonment are considerably negated by the crime-enhancing ones.
http://www.doc.state.ok.us/DOCS/OCJRC/Ocjrc96/Ocjrc7.htm

FAMILIES AGAINST MANDATORY
MINIMUMS FOUNDATION (FAMM FOUNDATION)

Families against Mandatory Minimums Foundation (FAMM Foundation) is a national organization of citizens working to reform federal and state mandatory sentencing laws that remove judicial discretion. To ensure equity and fairness at all stages of the sentencing process, FAMM works to improve sentencing guidelines. To accomplish their goal, FAMM educates the public and policymakers about mandatory sentences through media outreach, grassroots campaigns, and direct action. FAMM does not argue that crime should go unpunished—but that the punishment should fit the crime.
http://www.famm.org

U.S. SENTENCING COMMISSION

This informative site contains links, publications, reports to Congress, federal sentencing statistics, and information on state sentencing commissions.
http://www.ussc.gov

HUMAN RIGHTS 95

Human Rights 95 is a photo project/exhibit dedicated to those convicted of drug offenses and their families who are working to regain their freedom. The site contains case studies—including photos and stories—provided by nonviolent prisoners of the drug war who feel their penalties are unjust.
http://www.hr95.org

8

Is It Fair for Police to Use Racial Profiling When Targeting Suspects?

Historically, law enforcement in America has been used to control African Americans. During slavery, African Americans were minimally protected by law and were severely punished by it. After emancipation, African Americans were still unprotected from lynchings and abuse. Some see today's criminal justice system as being used for the disproportionate arrest and imprisonment of African-American men. More than one in three young African-American men are under criminal supervision nationwide. More young African-American men nationwide are in prison than in college.

Others have been more interested in the startlingly disproportionate racial victimization statistics. Black males experience robberies at more than twice the rate of white males; black females have a robbery rate three times that of white females. Blacks experience higher rates of violent crime, and those crimes cause greater injury than similar crimes against other races.

As part of a policy of crime control, various police departments have engaged in what has come to be known as "racial profiling," the police practice of using race as a factor in deciding whom to place under suspicion and/or surveillance. Cops see racial profiling as a statistically-based tool that enables them to focus their energies efficiently for the purpose of providing protection against crime. To borrow a concept from economics, it lowers the cost of obtaining and processing information, which in turn lowers the overall cost of doing the business of policing. Moreover, the fact that a number of cops who support racial profiling are black buttresses their claims that the practice isn't motivated by bigotry.

The police claim that there is no use pretending that blacks and whites commit crimes (or are victims of crime) in exact proportion to their respective shares of the population. Statistics confirm that African Americans—and particularly young African-American men—commit a disproportionate share of street crime in the United States. This, they claim, is a sociological fact, not a figment of the media's (or the police's) racist imagination.

Arch Puddington, in "The War on the War on Crime," argues that by its very nature, effective law enforcement will always be concentrated in high-crime neighborhoods, which in a city like New York means minority neighborhoods. This in itself suggests the emptiness of the charge that the NYPD engages in systematic "racial profiling." If minority communities are to be properly protected, the stop-and-frisks must take place in those communities.

Puddington claims that it is a measure of today's climate of political correctness that such a simple, commonsense observation can put one at risk of denunciation for racism. If those who believe that the police, not the criminals, pose the major threat in New York are permitted to succeed in their campaign to undo what has been accomplished over the past years, those in black and Hispanic neighborhoods will pay the highest price of all.

Randall Kennedy, in "Suspect Policy: Racial Profiling Usually Isn't Racist; It Can Help Stop Crime; and It Should Be Abolished," explains that the issue of racial profiling is more complex. Courts have agreed that the Constitution does not prohibit police from routinely taking race into account when they decide whom to stop and question, as long as they do so for purposes of bona fide law enforcement (not racial harassment) and as long as race is one of several factors that they consider.

Kennedy believes that defenders of racial profiling frequently neglect the costs of the practice. They unduly minimize (or ignore altogether) the large extent to which racial profiling constantly adds to the sense of resentment felt by blacks of every social stratum toward the law enforcement establishment. Ironically, this is a cost of racial profiling that may well hamper law enforcement.

Kennedy believes that racial profiling undercuts the idea that individuals should be judged by the police on the basis of their own conduct and not on the basis—not even partly on the basis—of racial generalizations.

Yes

Arch
Puddington

The War on the War on Crime

In the post-midnight hours of February 4 [1999], a young immigrant named Amadou Diallo from the African country of Guinea was about to enter his Bronx apartment building when he was approached by four plainclothes New York City police officers. The police were looking for a serial rapist who had assaulted some 40 women in minority neighborhoods in the Bronx and northern Manhattan. According to press accounts, the officers believed that Diallo bore a resemblance to sketch drawings of the rapist. What transpired next—whether the police identified themselves, whether Diallo understood them, whether his movements led them to conclude he was reaching for a weapon—has still not been made clear. There is no question, however, about the reaction of the police. All four drew their guns and fired a total of 41 shots. Nineteen bullets struck Diallo, killing him instantly.

...

Within minutes, if not seconds, the four officers discovered they had made a terrible mistake. Diallo was unarmed; his pockets contained only keys and a beeper. A subsequent investigation would reveal that he had no police record. Although, in order to gain admission to the United States, he had falsely claimed to have been persecuted in Mauritania, he was otherwise an upstanding young man who worked long hours as a street vendor while studying to acquire the high-school credits to enroll in an American university.

It did not take long before angry reactions to the shooting were voiced by the mayor's many critics.... There were protests at the Bronx courthouse where a grand jury was investigating the conduct of the police; acts of civil disobedience at a Wall Street brokerage firm; and demonstrations at City Hall

From *Commentary* (May 1, 1999). Copyright © 1999. Reprinted with the permission of the author and *Commentary*. All rights reserved.

featuring speeches by "representatives" of violent youth gangs like the Crips, Bloods, and Latin Kings. For weeks, the city witnessed one staged event after another in a choreographed drive to show that black New York was in a state of outrage.

...

The specific object of the protesters' wrath was the New York City Police Department—and, by extension, the city's criminal justice system as a whole.... The Reverend Jesse Jackson compared the Diallo case to the lynching of Emmitt Till, a young black man whose death at the hands of a Mississippi mob in the 1950s became an emblem of Southern racial injustice. The same analogy was employed by Ira Glasser, director of the American Civil Liberties Union (ACLU), who declared Amadou Diallo the victim of "Jim Crow justice."

The agent of this system of Jim Crow justice was said to be New York's much-publicized crackdown on "quality-of-life" offenses.... For several years now, this strategy has seen the daily arrest of hundreds of New Yorkers for drinking or smoking marijuana in public, subway-fare beating, reckless bicycle riding, and the like; it has also brought to light huge numbers of concealed and illegal weapons, often in the hands of people with outstanding warrants for more serious offenses. The most zealous prosecutors of the new policy have been the members of NYPD's street-crime unit, an elite group of undercover officers deployed in high-crime neighborhoods. Given a broad mandate to take measures to stop crime before it occurs, officers in this unit (among their number were the four who shot Diallo) scour the streets seeking out those who prey on cab drivers, prostitutes, and small businessmen.

...

[I]n 1997 and 1998, the unit stopped and searched some 45,000 people, primarily in minority neighborhoods; arrests were made only in some 9,500 cases. To black and Hispanic politicians, these figures suggest that large numbers of innocent people are being singled out for random and arbitrary abuse. The name given to this abuse is *racial* profiling," i.e., deliberately targeting nonwhites for stop-and-search encounters without reasonable grounds for suspicion.

...

As for the four officers in the Diallo case, who have been indicted by a grand jury on second-degree murder charges, no evidence has been put forward to support the repeated charge that they acted out of racism. It is true that all four are white, and that one of them had previously been involved in the shooting of a suspect but has since been cleared. Otherwise, there seems to be nothing unusual or incriminating in their backgrounds—no reports of racial prejudice, no charges of brutality, nothing to suggest that they have been anything but model officers. Indeed, eyewitnesses at the shooting scene described the four as dazed and anguished at discovering they had killed an unarmed man, and all of them were hospitalized for trauma on the night of the incident.

This is hardly to deny that New York, like all cities, continues to experience controversial instances of police shootings, or that such shootings often involve white officers and black or Hispanic youths. Given the disproportionate involvement of the latter groups in street crimes, however, that is as inevitable as it is unfortunate. Completely ignored in the post-Diallo furor was the fact that, while blacks make up 13 percent of the American population, they comprise over half the arrests for murder and robbery, over 40 percent of the arrests for rape and car theft, and over 30 percent for burglary. These are national figures; for New York, the figures are even higher.

By its very nature, effective law enforcement will always be concentrated in high-crime neighborhoods, which in a city like New York means minority neighborhoods. This in itself suggests the emptiness of the charge that the NYPD engages in systematic "racial profiling." As Michael Hess, the city's chief attorney, has frankly and truthfully put it, "If minority communities are to be properly protected, the stop-and-frisks must take place in those communities."

It is a measure of today's climate of political correctness that such a simple, commonsense observation can put one at risk of denunciation for racism. Indeed, just weeks after the Diallo incident, the New Jersey state police chief, Carl A. Williams, was forced from office for speaking in an interview about the link between certain ethnic groups and the drug trade. To New Jersey's civil-rights leadership, his remarks were clear evidence of a racist mindset— "the tip of the iceberg," in the words of one black state legislator, "of the apparent racist administration of the state police." Governor Christine Todd Whitman dismissed Williams the day after the interview was published.

What had Williams said? Only that it was naive to think the police could effectively enforce laws against drug trafficking without taking into account the ethnicity of those who control the narcotics trade. "Two weeks ago the President of the United States went to Mexico to talk to the president of Mexico about drugs," Williams noted. "He didn't go to Ireland. He didn't go to England." Williams then provided an equal-opportunity list of the groups involved in this activity. Trade in methamphetamines, he said, was controlled by white motorcycle gangs; Jamaicans dominated heroin traffic; American blacks and certain Hispanic and Caribbean groups led in the smuggling of marijuana and cocaine.

Williams's comments were not made on the basis of prejudice. His identification of particular ethnic groups with particular aspects of the drug trade was taken virtually verbatim from a study that had been compiled by the various federal agencies involved in the enforcement of drug laws and that was submitted by the Drug Enforcement Agency (DEA) to the White House in 1996, where it was received without a word of criticism. By the standards of today's racial debate, the Clinton administration's DEA report might itself be deemed a prime example of racial profiling. Of course, it is but a statement of fact.

Another consideration is relevant here, though it too has been sedulously ignored. This is that polling data show many black Americans inclined to see racism not only among the police but in virtually every aspect of American life. A disturbing percentage believes that the AIDS virus was invented to decimate the black population, that crack cocaine was introduced into the black community by a white conspiracy involving the Central Intelligence Agency, and that there is a white plot to destroy young black men. Even blacks who reject such paranoid fantasies often claim to see prejudice behind the casual phrase of a co-worker, a teacher's body language, or a store owner's abrupt manner.

Under these circumstances, it is hardly surprising that blacks should be convinced they are the targets of a pervasive form of police racism, and in particular that the stop-and-frisk tactics employed by the street-crime unit have been designed to humiliate the innocent rather than to snare the criminal. Such sentiments are reinforced by the indiscriminate anti-police rhetoric voiced by Jesse Jackson and other black leaders.

...

If the critics' diagnosis of the NYPD problems is without merit, so too are the remedies on offer. One such remedy ... is mandatory ethnic sensitivity training for all members of the police force. This idea, perhaps harmless in itself, is also nonsensical. New York is home to over 100 ethnic and immigrant groups.... Just as no course in sensitivity training could hope to acquaint police officers with the wildly disparate styles they are likely to encounter in the course of a week's patrol, there is little chance that sensitivity training would be of any use whatsoever in crisis situations requiring a split-second decision to shoot or not to shoot.

A more serious proposal is to step up affirmative-action programs within the NYPD itself, with the aim of recruiting more officers from minority communities. Another, reflecting the same impulse, is to require police officers to live in the city they serve.

...

Other things being equal, it is no doubt desirable that a police force broadly reflect the racial and ethnic makeup of the community it patrols. But there is no evidence at all that affirmative action actually improves the quality of police work; that minority police officers are less prone to misconduct than white officers; or that police who live in the city or the neighborhood they patrol are more effective than police who live in the suburbs. The New York Civilian Complaint Review Board has received proportionately the same number of complaints filed by minority citizens against minority officers as by minority citizens against white officers. Worse still, cities like Detroit and Washington, D.C. that have undertaken highly aggressive affirmative-action programs have experienced problems with misconduct and incompetence as standards have been lowered to bring minority officers into the ranks.

This, however, is another of today's taboo subjects—which is why one would be hard put to name a single instance in which the killing or beating of innocent black civilians by black officers has been made an object of press scrutiny or organized protest. Several years ago, a black officer shot and killed a young boy while patrolling a Brooklyn housing project. Residents described the officer as nervous and quick to draw his gun, but the story died after a few days with no demands for a grand-jury investigation or—needless to say—Justice Department intervention, and no demonstrations of outrage....

...

But in the movement sparked by the Diallo affair, a larger agenda is being advanced as well, one that threatens to have the most baneful consequences not only for the city in general but for its minority inhabitants in particular. Pushing this agenda are liberals unhappy with the direction of law enforcement under Giuliani and convinced, against a mountain of evidence to the contrary, that the way to fight crime is to direct one's energies not at crime itself but at its alleged "root causes" in poverty and racism.

Over the past decade or so, root-cause liberals, to borrow the term of the criminologist George L. Kelling, have been on the defensive. New techniques of policing, techniques that they opposed at every turn, have proved wonderfully effective in reducing urban violent crime. Now, with the Diallo affair, root-cause liberals see a chance to press for a reversal of current policies and simultaneously to destroy the elected official most closely identified with them.

...

In the 1960s and 70s, black radicals and their white liberal sympathizers, aided by a series of Supreme Court decisions significantly broadening the legal rights of criminal defendants, successfully intimidated any politicians who dared raise concerns about street crime. In this atmosphere, law-enforcement authorities themselves began to express defeatist attitudes, to believe and even to act as if the war on crime could never be won.

A legal and cultural transformation was required before the results of this breakdown could at last begin to be undone. But it was not until the late 1980s and early 1990s, thanks in large part to the election of a new breed of urban mayors, that a change came to be registered in the ever-climbing rates of murders, assaults, rapes, and other violent offenses devastating America's cities. Although the tale has been told often enough, perhaps the most important consequence of the new and more assertive war on crime ... is still not sufficiently appreciated: namely, the massive decrease in violent crime in minority neighborhoods.

This is again a national phenomenon, but again New York led the way. If murders committed with a firearm in New York City dropped from an all-time high of 1,605 in 1991 to 375 in 1998—a decline of 77 percent—in the precinct where Amadou Diallo lived, murders were down by a stunning 81 percent. Similar figures have been recorded in other neighborhoods whose very names were once synonymous with violent crime. Although one would hardly know it from the avalanche of condemnation it has evoked in the wake of the Diallo affair, the NYPD street-crime unit played a central role in this drastic reduction.

Around the time of the Diallo shooting, it was announced that, for the first time in years, all five boroughs of New York City were experiencing an increase in population. This development, attributable in large measure to the civility and order that have been restored to the city's streets ..., is a vivid reminder of the high stakes involved in the current debate over race and law enforcement. In the avalanche of anti-police invective, it is easy to forget that today, for the first time in decades, law-abiding minority citizens can go shopping, visit friends, or conduct business in an environment of relative security. The measure of order now prevailing in Harlem, the South Bronx, and other neighborhoods that not long ago were completely written off has laid a foundation for the economic revival they are now experiencing.

If those who believe that the police, not the criminals, pose the major threat in New York are permitted to succeed in their campaign to undo what has been accomplished over the last years, all New Yorkers will pay a price, but black and Hispanic neighborhoods will pay the highest price of all.... [A]s the street-crime unit backed off its assertive tactics in the wake of the post-Diallo protests, crime and murder rates in minority neighborhoods shot up again. This and much worse is what awaits unless those determined to drag us back into the anarchy of the past are firmly repudiated.

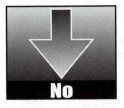

Suspect Policy: Racial Profiling Usually Isn't Racist; It Can Help Stop Crime; and It Should Be Abolished

Randall
Kennedy

Consider the following case study in the complex interaction of race and law enforcement. An officer from the Drug Enforcement Administration stops and questions a young man who has just stepped off a flight to Kansas City from Los Angeles. The officer has focused on this man for several reasons. Intelligence reports indicate that black gangs in Los Angeles are flooding the Kansas City area with illegal drugs, and the man in question was on a flight originating in Los Angeles. Young, toughly dressed, and appearing very nervous, he paid for his ticket in cash, checked no luggage, brought two carry-on bags, and made a beeline for a taxi upon deplaning. Oh, and one other thing: the officer also took into account the fact that the young man was black. When asked to explain himself, the officer declares that he considered the individual's race, along with other factors, because doing so helps him efficiently allocate the limited time and other resources at his disposal.

How should we evaluate the officer's conduct? Should we applaud it? Permit it? Prohibit it? As you think through this example, be aware that it is not a hypothetical one. Encounters like this take place every day, all over the country, as police attempt to battle street crime, drug trafficking, and illegal immigration. And this particular case study happens to be the fact pattern presented in a federal lawsuit of the early '90s, *United States v. Weaver*, in which the U.S. Court of Appeals for the Eighth Circuit upheld the constitutionality of the officer's action.

"Large groups of our citizens," the court declared, "should not be regarded by law enforcement officers as presumptively criminal based upon

From *The New Republic* (September 19, 1999). Copyright © 1999 by The New Republic, Inc. Reprinted with the permission of the publishers.

their race." The court went on to say, however, that "facts are not to be ignored simply because they may be unpleasant." According to the court, the
circumstances were such that it made sense for the officer to regard blackness,
when considered in conjunction with the other factors, as a signal that could
be legitimately relied upon in the decision to approach and ultimately detain
the suspect. "We wish it were otherwise," the court maintained, "but we take
the facts as they are presented to us, not as we would like them to be." Other
courts have agreed with the Eighth Circuit that the Constitution does not
prohibit police from routinely taking race into account when they decide
whom to stop and question, as long as they do so for purposes of bona fide
law enforcement (not racial harassment) and as long as race is one of several factors that they consider.

These judicial decisions have been welcome news to the many police officers and other law enforcement officials who consider the racial selectivity
of the sort deployed by the DEA agent an essential weapon in the war on
crime. Such defenders of what has come to be known as racial profiling maintain that, in areas where young African-American males commit a disproportionate number of the street crimes, the cops are justified in scrutinizing
that sector of the population more closely than others—just as they are generally justified in scrutinizing men more closely than women.

…

For cops … racial profiling is a sensible, statistically based tool that enables them to focus their energies efficiently for the purpose of providing protection against crime to law-abiding folk. To borrow a concept from economics,
it lowers the cost of obtaining and processing information, which in turn lowers the overall cost of doing the business of policing.

Moreover, the very fact that a number of cops who support racial profiling are black, like Parks, buttresses their claims that the practice isn't motivated by bigotry. Indeed, these police officers note that racial profiling is
race-neutral in that various forms of it can be applied to persons of all races,
depending on the circumstances. In predominantly black neighborhoods and
other places in which white people stick out in a suspiciously anomalous
fashion (as potential drug customers or racist hooligans, for example), whiteness can become part of a profile. In the southwestern United States, where
Latinos often traffic in illegal immigrants, apparent Latin American ancestry
can become part of a profile. In a Chinatown where Chinese gangs appear to
dominate certain criminal rackets, apparent Chinese ancestry can become
part of a profile. Racial profiling, then, according to many cops, is good police work: a race-neutral, empirically based, and, above all, effective tool in
fighting crime.

…

Unfortunately, though, many who condemn racial profiling do so
without really thinking the issue through. One common complaint about
racial profiling is that using race (say, blackness) as one of several factors in

selecting targets of surveillance is fundamentally and necessarily racist. But racial selectivity of this sort can be defended on nonracist grounds and is, in fact, embraced by people who are by no means anti-black bigots and are not even cops. Even Jesse Jackson once revealed himself to be an amateur racial profiler. "There is nothing more painful to me at this stage in my life," he said in 1993, "than to walk down the street and hear footsteps and start to think about robbery and then look around and see somebody white and feel relieved." The reason Jackson felt relief was not that he dislikes black people. He felt relief because he estimated, probably correctly, that he stood a somewhat greater risk of being robbed by a black person than by a white person.

A second standard criticism of racial profiling involves a blanket denial of the central empirical claim upon which the practice rests: that in certain jurisdictions individuals associated with particular racial groups commit a disproportionate number of the crimes. But there's no use pretending that blacks and whites commit crimes (or are victims of crime) in exact proportion to their respective shares of the population. Statistics abundantly confirm that African Americans—and particularly young black men—commit a dramatically disproportionate share of street crime in the United States. This is a sociological fact, not a figment of the media's (or the police's) racist imaginations. In recent years, for example, victims of crime report blacks as the perpetrators in around 25 percent of the violent crimes suffered, although blacks constitute only about 12 percent of the nation's population.

So, if racial profiling isn't necessarily bigoted, and if the empirical claim upon which the practice rests is sound, why is it wrong?

The argument begins with an insistence upon the special significance of racial distinctions in American life and law. Racial distinctions are and should be different from other lines of social stratification. That is why, since the civil rights revolution of the 1960s, courts have typically ruled—pursuant to the Fourteenth Amendment's equal protection clause—that mere reasonableness is an insufficient justification for officials to discriminate on racial grounds. In such cases, courts have generally insisted on applying "strict scrutiny"— the most intense level of judicial review—to the government's actions. Under this tough standard, the use of race in governmental decision making may be upheld only if it serves a compelling government objective and only if it is "narrowly tailored" to advance that objective. Strict scrutiny embodies the recognition, forged in the difficult crucible of American history, that the presence of a racial factor in governmental decision making gives rise to the presumption that officials may be acting in violation of someone's civil rights.

A disturbing feature of the debate over racial profiling is that many people, including judges, are suggesting that decisions distinguishing between persons on a racial basis do not constitute unlawful racial discrimination when race is not the sole consideration prompting disparate treatment. The court that upheld the DEA agent's detainment of the young black man at the Kansas City airport declined to describe the agent's action as racially discriminatory and thus evaded the requirement of subjecting the government's action to strict scrutiny.... [W]hen race is just one of a number of factors, the profiling ceases to be "racial" and becomes instead a defensible technique in which a police officer merely uses "cumulative knowledge and training to identify certain indicators of possible criminal activity." This dilution of the meaning of discrimination is troubling not only because it permits racial profiling to continue without adequate scrutiny. Even worse, this confusion will likely seep into other areas of racial controversy, causing mischief along the way.

Few racially discriminatory decisions are animated by only one motivation; they typically stem from mixed motives. For example, an employer who prefers white candidates to black candidates—except black candidates with clearly superior experience and test scores—is engaging in racial discrimination, even though race is not the only factor he considers (since he is willing to select black superstars). There are, of course, different degrees of discrimination. In some cases, race is a marginal factor; in others it is the only factor. The distinction may have a bearing on the moral or logical justification for the discrimination. But it cannot logically negate the existence of racial discrimination. Taking race into account at all means engaging in racial discrimination.

Because racial discrimination is discouraged by both law and morality, proponents of racial profiling should bear the burden of persuading the public that such discrimination is justifiable. Instead, defenders of racial profiling frequently neglect the costs of the practice. They unduly minimize (or ignore altogether) the large extent to which racial profiling constantly adds to the sense of resentment felt by blacks of every social stratum toward the law enforcement establishment. Ironically, this is a cost of racial profiling that may well hamper law enforcement. In the immediate aftermath of O. J. Simpson's acquittal, when blacks' accumulated anger at and distrust of the criminal justice system became frighteningly clear, there existed a widespread recognition of the danger that threatens all Americans when cynicism and rage suffuse a substantial sector of the country. Alienation of that sort gives rise to witnesses who fail to cooperate with the police, citizens who view prosecutors as "the enemy," lawyers who disdain the rules they have sworn to uphold, and jurors who yearn to "get even" with a system that has, in their eyes, consistently mistreated them. For the sake of better law enforcement, we need to be mindful of the deep reservoir of anger toward the police that now exists within many racial minority neighborhoods. Racial profiling is a big part of what keeps this pool of accumulated rage filled to the brim.

...

My case against racial profiling concludes on a frankly ideological note. Racial profiling undercuts a good idea that needs more support from both society and the law: that individuals should be judged by public authority on the basis of their own conduct and not on the basis—not even partly on the basis—of racial generalization. Race-dependent policing retards the development and spread of such thinking; indeed, it encourages the opposite tendency.

What about the fact that in some jurisdictions it is demonstrable that people associated with a given racial group commit a disproportionately large number of the crimes? Our commitment to a just social order should prompt us to end racial profiling even if the generalizations on which the technique is based are buttressed by empirical evidence. This is not as unusual as it may sound. There are actually many contexts in which the law properly enjoins us to forswear the playing of racial odds even when doing so would advance certain legitimate goals.

For example, public opinion surveys have established that blacks tend to be more distrustful than whites of law enforcement. Thus, for purposes of convicting certain defendants, it would be rational—and not necessarily racist—for a prosecutor to use race as a factor in seeking to exclude black potential jurors. Fortunately, the Supreme Court has outlawed racial discrimination of this sort. Similarly, it is a demographic fact that whites tend to live longer than blacks. Therefore, it would be perfectly rational for insurers to charge blacks higher life-insurance premiums than whites. Fortunately, though, the law forbids that, too. And, given that, statistically, whites tend to be better educated than blacks, it might make business sense for an employer to give a racial edge to white applicants. But a battery of laws proscribes racial discrimination in the workplace, even under circumstances in which it would strengthen a business's bottom line.

The point here is that racial equality, like all good things in life, costs something; it does not come for free. Politicians often speak as if all that Americans need to do in order to attain racial justice is forswear bigotry. They must do that. But they must do more as well. They must be willing to demand equal treatment before the law even under circumstances in which unequal treatment is plausibly defensible in the name of nonracist goals. They must even be willing to do so when their effort will be costly.

Since abandoning racial profiling would undeniably raise the information costs of policing to some extent, with some attendant potential loss in effective crime control, those of us who would do away with it must advocate a responsible alternative. Mine is simply to spend more on other means of enforcement—and then spread the cost on some nonracial basis. This is hardly infeasible. One possibility is hiring more police officers. Another is subjecting everyone to closer surveillance. A benefit of the second option would be to acquaint more whites with the burden of police intrusion, the knowledge of which might prompt more whites to insist upon reining the police in. As it stands now, this burden falls with unfair severity upon minorities—imposing on Mexican Americans, blacks, and others a special kind of tax for the war against illegal immigration, drugs, and other forms of criminality. The racial character of that tax should be repealed.

I am not saying that police should never be able to refer to race. If a young white man with blue hair robs me, the police should certainly be able to use the description of the perpetrator's race in efforts to apprehend the felon. In this situation, though, whiteness is a trait linked to a particular person with respect to a particular incident. It is not a free-floating proxy for risk that hovers over young white men practically all the time—which is the predicament in which young black men currently find themselves. Nor am I saying absolutely that race could never be legitimately relied upon as a signal of increased danger. In an extraordinary circumstance in which plausible alternatives appear to be absent, officials might appropriately feel bound to resort to racial profiling. This would be right, however, only in a rare instance in which a strong presumption against racial profiling has been overcome by evidence of compelling circumstances. This is a far cry from the situation today, in which racial profiling is routine and is subjected to far less scrutiny than it warrants.

...

Unfortunately, though, a minefield of complexity occupies the terrain beneath many of these actions—which, after all, have been spurred by politicians' simplistic rhetoric. Unless these complexities are understood, this fleeting opportunity to address racial profiling properly will be wasted. Take the basic issue of defining racial profiling. As we have seen, many police officials, politicians, and community activists say that racial profiling occurs when a police officer stops, questions, or arrests someone solely on the basis of his or her skin color. They propose that definition for different reasons. Community activists like it because it helps them fire up the emotions of their followers by evoking a scene that is unequivocally evil: the crudely bigoted officer, to gratify his or her racist itch, harassing and humiliating black men for no legitimate purpose. Police officials and politicians like this definition, too, because it enables them to condemn resoundingly something that is already thoroughly discredited.

To fulminate against police officers who engage in such practices, however, requires no real confrontation with the status quo, because hardly anyone of substance or standing defends police surveillance triggered solely by race. The legal system stands ready to punish the officer who uses race alone as a signal of suspicion. Attacking this version of racial profiling is like attacking the racially motivated burning of churches. It is fine as long as one acknowledges that the target of the condemnation is, in the overall scheme of things, a rather marginal phenomenon. It is not so fine insofar as such rhetoric deepens public confusion. Much of the talk about police "targeting" of suspects on the basis of race is, in this sense, misguided and harmful. It diverts attention from the major part of the story to a side issue.

The better definition of racial profiling embraces a much more wide-spread police practice: using race as a factor in deciding whom to place under suspicion and/or surveillance. Relatively few police officers detain a person solely on the basis of race.... Much more typical is questioning or detaining a person because of the confluence of a variety of factors—age (young), dress (hooded sweatshirt, baggy pants, etc.), time (late evening), geography (the person is walking through the "wrong" neighborhood)—that include race (black). It is the confluence of such factors that constitutes the profile that triggers police attention. Properly understood, then, racial profiling occurs whenever police routinely use race as a negative signal that, along with an accumulation of other signals, causes an officer to react with suspicion.

Thus, we must be skeptical and realistic as we watch and participate in the growing debate over racial profiling. One danger that I have already mentioned is the threat of demagoguery through oversimplification. When politicians discuss "racial profiling," we must insist that they define precisely what they mean and ask in particular whether they merely reject police surveillance based solely on race or whether they also condemn police surveillance that is at all triggered by a racial factor (except in the exceptional circumstances I have noted). Another danger is evasion—putting off making hard decisions in the guise of needing more information. This motivation, I fear, is behind Clinton's directive ordering federal agencies to gather statistics on the racial demographics of stops, questionings, and arrests. There is no mystery about whether federal and state police agencies use race routinely in making determinations of suspicion. Officials have said repeatedly that they do. The issue is whether the Clinton administration is willing to go beyond easy rhetoric and actually direct federal law enforcement personnel to cease their routine use of race as a factor in selecting subjects to scrutinize or question. On this point, Bradley was right when he criticized Gore for promising to end racial profiling only after he's elected president. The Clinton-Gore administration does not need to wait for court rulings or legislation or more data. It can and should act now. True, the federal government's law enforcement agencies are smaller than the combined forces of local and state authorities. But the DEA, the FBI, the Border Patrol, and other federal agencies are still important. And state and local cops often emulate their policies.

Finally, it must be soberly acknowledged that, even if this or any other administration does prohibit routine racial profiling, the practice will not cease quickly. After all, it will be difficult to prove that an officer made a given decision on a partly racial basis if he or she keeps silent regarding the racial aspect of his or her decisions and mentions, when pressed, only the nonracial cues. Moreover, supervisors and judges would probably be loath to reject an officer's proffered nonracial explanation. For one thing, doing so would typically lead not only to concluding that an officer acted on an unlawful basis but also, generally, to ruling that the officer lied about his or her conduct. Generalized avoidance of such confrontations is a fact of social psychology—albeit one that enables a considerable amount of illegal racial discrimination to pass undisturbed.

Even so, it would be helpful … to promulgate a strict anti-discrimination directive now. That would at least send a signal to conscientious, law-abiding officers that there are certain criteria they ought not to use. If nothing else, it might force racial profiling into the realm of conduct that officers may practice on the sly but don't dare admit to. To be sure, it's not optimal to create a norm that can't be fully enforced. But even if it can't be, that should just encourage us all to work that much harder to close the lingering gap between our laws and the actual conduct of those in positions of public authority. Even if a new rule against racial profiling would, to some degree, be made to be broken, it would still be worth having—for it would at least help set a new standard for legitimate government.

KEY WEBSITES

BLACK SKIN, WHITE JUSTICE: RACE MATTERS IN THE CRIMINAL JUSTICE SYSTEM

Gary Highsmith, "Black Skin, White Justice: Race Matters in the Criminal Justice System": Highsmith designed this teaching unit for social studies, law, sociology, or Black history students, to explore the significance of race in the criminal justice system. Highsmith believes the U.S. criminal justice system has frequently been biased against black people. He notes that black people in America are facing a serious crisis in regards to their involvement in the criminal justice system, and this crisis manifests itself at every level of interaction with this system.
http://www.yale.edu/ynhti/curriculum/units/1996/1/96.01.10.x. html

DRIVING WHILE BLACK: RACIAL PROFILING ON OUR NATION'S HIGHWAYS—AN AMERICAN CIVIL LIBERTIES UNION SPECIAL REPORT

David A. Harris, "Driving While Black: Racial Profiling on Our Nation's Highways—An American Civil Liberties Union Special Report," June 1999: One of the ACLU's highest priority issues is the fight against the practice of racial profiling. This report documents the practice of substituting skin color for evidence as a grounds for suspicion by law enforcement officials. The ACLU believes racial profiling police stops have reached epidemic proportions in recent years—fueled by the "War on Drugs" that has given police a pretext to target people who they think fit a "drug courier" or "gang member" profile. This website is designed to educate the public and enlist citizens in the fight to end racial profiling in America.
http://www.aclu.org/profiling/report/index.html

THE SENTENCING PROJECT—DRUG POLICY AND THE CRIMINAL JUSTICE SYSTEM

The Sentencing Project, incorporated in 1986, has become a national leader in the development of alternative sentencing programs and in the reform of criminal justice policy. The Sentencing Project has provided technical assistance and helped to establish alternative sentencing programs in more than 20 states. These programs provide judges with a broad range of sentencing options that have resulted in the diversion of offenders from incarceration by making effective use of community resources and supervision. The Sentencing Project website is designed to provide resources and information for the news media and a public concerned with criminal justice and sentencing issues.
http://www.sentencingproject.org/brief/5047.htm

THE COLOR OF SUSPICION

Jeffrey Goldberg, "The Color of Suspicion," *New York Times* Magazine, June 20, 1999: The way cops perceive blacks—and how those perceptions shape and misshape crime fighting—is now the most charged racial issue in America. The systematic harassment of black drivers has brought the relationship between blacks and cops to a level of seemingly irreversible toxicity. Neither side understands the other. The innocent black man, humiliated during a stop-and-frisk or a pretext car stop, asks: Whatever happened to the Fourth Amendment? It is no wonder, blacks say, that the police are so wildly mistrusted. And then there's the cop, who says: Why shouldn't I look at race when I'm looking for crime? It is no state secret that blacks commit a disproportionate amount of crime, so "racial profiling" is simply good police work. From the front seat of a police cruiser, racial profiling is a tool—and cops have no intention of giving it up.
http://www.nytimes.com/library/magazine/home/19990620
mag-race-cops.html

THE BLACK PEOPLE'S PRISON SURVIVAL GUIDE

This is a self-help survival guide to help "the reader safeguard his or her mental, physical, and spiritual well-being while in prison." The author of this book has been imprisoned in Ohio for the past 15 years, for a crime that he admits he committed. He says, "Experience is the most qualified teacher, and I have been well-schooled by my past experience with prisons and people in them."
http://www.cs.oberlin.edu/students/pjaques/etext/
prison-guide.html

**Alamance Community College
Library
P.O. Box 8000
Graham, NC 27253**